The Philosopher's Beach Book

The
Philosopher's
Beach Book

MEL THOMPSON

HODDER
EDUCATION

Hodder Education

338 Euston Road, London NW1 3BH.

Hodder Education is an Hachette UK company

First published in UK 2012 by Hodder Education

This edition published 2012.

www.hoddereducation.co.uk

Cover image ©

Typeset by Cenveo Publisher Services.

Printed and bound by CPI Group (UK) Ltd, Croydon, CR0 4YY.

Also available in ebook

Contents

Introduction: Your 'beach' opportunity

A holiday beach is a strange phenomenon. For the ancient Hebrews, the sea symbolized chaos; the deep out of whose dark depths the world had originally been created, the home of Leviathan, an unformed, threatening and untamed mantle thrown round the solid earth. It was something to be approached with trepidation. Yet observe a holiday resort and you see people turning their backs on the land of their everyday life. They sit on a beach and stare out over the sea to a near-featureless horizon, lulled by the sound of the waves into a soporific state in which even the arrival of a seagull becomes a significant event. Flesh creamed and eyes shaded, they lie out in rows, absorbing the warmth of the sun, seeking to avoid the sensory overload of home and work by luxuriating in just a few sensations. They attempt to relax and clear their minds.

Whereas at home they would choose to eat on a clean table, here they are prepared to risk getting sand in their sandwiches. The comfortable sofa is exchanged for the folding chair, a blanket or simply a stretch of sand hopefully free from litter or the needs of the doggy fraternity. They are drawn out here to the margins of something into which they can (literally or metaphorically) do little more than dip their toes. They may, of course, paddle boats on it, windsurf, water or jet ski across it, entertainingly skimming the surface. For some, the snorkel or scuba kit take them further away from the land, immersing them in a wonderful world which has not been their natural home since the first amphibians crawled out onto the land

400 million years ago. Few would choose to venture further down into the sea's murky depths and it only takes a few seconds of rhythmic bowing from cellos and basses to remind us of *Jaws*.

All human life is here. People parade up and down through the shallow water – observing or keen to be observed. The beach is a place for sexual display. It is also the place where the sheer variety of human physicality dampens sexual ardour. Little knots of people, burning in the sun or shivering in the cold, stand staring out to sea, while around them children amuse themselves by moving sand from one place to another, and creating castles that the tide will soon overwhelm – providing them with a valuable and necessary image of life. Next to them, parents stand and stare, and perhaps wonder how they can defend their own domestic sandcastles against the inevitable tide of time.

But if the beach is, for the purpose of our title, used as an image of what a holiday is all about, it certainly does not exhaust that phenomenon. Nowadays we take adventure holidays, climb mountains, struggle with foreign languages, try new foods (although a diminishing possibility in a world where diet is globalized). We may choose to take to a canal, throbbing along in a narrow boat at 4 miles an hour, until the rhythm of the diesel engine soothes us into a relaxed state in which every moorhen crossing the canal commands our willing attention.

But whether you are backpacking, engaging in life-threatening activities, or simply sitting by beach or pool, holidays provide you with an opportunity to stand back from your life, consider who you are, and perhaps make resolutions about what you will do on your return. It is a time when relationships are threatened (rivalled only by the stress of Christmas) or love re-affirmed, when families come together or blow apart. It is a time of heightened awareness. When did you last spend time just staring at a beautiful scene? It is a time when you can 'be yourself' or (if you don't much like yourself) pretend to be someone else.

It is an opportunity to think about who you are, what you believe and what you want to do with your life. It gives a longer perspective on your work, your family, your values. It may be the wine, the heat, the fact that my mind is freed from routine hassle, but it seems to me that holidays are the ideal opportunity for a bit of non-routine thinking. And just as the slightly inebriated sense that they have glimpsed the meaning of life, even if they cannot articulate it when sober, so – with the mild inebriation that comes from being on holiday – we may find that our intuitions and thoughts give us insights that would not occur in the daily routine of home. Freed from everyday pressures, the mind sees things new.

But of course you don't need to be on holiday to benefit from a bit of distance. Problems often clarify only once we step back from them. Sleep on it, they say, with good reason. Take a break; stop the meeting; bring in the coffee; take a walk to clear the mind – we all need our 'beach' moments, when we relax and wait for a new set of ideas to arise.

If that's the way it is (or could be) for you, then you are in good company. Many of the greatest insights have come once the mind is removed from the routine. Archimedes is famously said to have jumped out of the bath shouting 'Eureka' – he had found it! Leaving aside the inevitable crude jokes, or the unlikely story that, in his excitement, he ran naked into the street in Syracuse, his moment of insight is instructive for us. His answer came when he stepped back from the problem of slicing shapes in order to calculate their volume, and had gone to take a bath. Archimedes had wrestled with the problem of finding the density of an irregular object – in this case a votive crown in which the gold had allegedly been replaced with an equal weight of silver. He knew the weight, but only the volume would tell him the density and thus if the crown were solid gold. The displacement of water in his bath gave him a practical solution to his problem. An alert mind in relaxed state is open to both intuition and ingenuity.

Sometimes it's a matter of finding the right place to relax. In 1637, the philosopher Descartes published his famous *Discourse on the Method of Rightly Conducting One's Reason and Seeking the Truth in the Sciences* – hardly a catchy title but absolutely to the point! At the opening of Part 2, he says that, while returning to the army (he had become a gentleman officer) after attending the coronation of the Emperor, he found himself delayed by winter weather in a small village in Germany where, with no other diversions, he spent the whole day shut up in a stove-heated room with leisure to pursue his own thoughts without distraction. Whether it was by that stove that he came up with his famous, indubitable claim 'I think, therefore I am' we cannot be certain. What we do know is that he sat there and quietly reviewed his habitual way of thinking, resolving to set all pre-conceived notions aside in his quest for certainty. The ideas he developed were to set a trend in philosophy that was to last for the next three centuries.

Finding the right spot to think is one thing, having the determination to stay there focused on one's philosophical questions is quite another. The Buddha sat beneath a Pipal tree and vowed that he would not move until he had discovered the secret of life and the cause of suffering. That does seem a bit drastic, but it clearly worked. After a night of struggling with all manner of distractions and temptations, his insight came with the dawn. This book will not necessarily recommend that you determine to stay on holiday until enlightenment comes!

One thing is certain; it's difficult to be creative when tired – the best ideas come, almost accidentally, when relaxed and receptive. So, to get an intellectual and personal focus on your life, what better place than the beach? Of course, there is no need to take this literally – your 'beach' may be a mountain track, a woodland walk or a deckchair in the back garden. You may be in five-star luxury or camping in the corner of some French farmer's field. You need not even be on holiday to find your 'beach' – it is just a metaphor for taking a break from the routine of life and asking yourself 'What do I really think? What makes sense? What am I looking for in life?'

These personal, existential questions are not, of course, the whole of philosophy. Much that is practised in university departments is highly abstract, analysing meaning, language and logic to a degree that would not be appropriate on a beach. But that does not imply that the more general, existential questions are any less important. Many of the ancient philosophers, from whom we have received the whole tradition of Western thought, were absolutely committed to the question of how we live and what is worthwhile. Plato, the Stoics, the

Epicureans, all expected philosophy to make a difference to ordinary life. And in modern times, philosophers such as Hume and Kierkegaard have clearly lived out their philosophy and others, particularly the existentialists, made the question of human significance and meaning primary. Marx was not the only thinker to argue that his task was not merely to understand the world but to change it. Every worthwhile philosophy presents a challenge, always intellectual but sometimes also personal and social.

But clear thinking requires a basic framework and questions to get it started. That is what this book seeks to offer you. Each short chapter will introduce a question; some of these will be more personal, others more abstract. All are designed to challenge habitual ways of thinking.

So this is the moment to dig your toes into the sand, put on your shades, and let your mind freewheel along the gentle undulations of an intellectual path.

01

Can a heap of sand prevent baldness?

Thanks to Eubulides of Miletus, a Greek philosopher from the 4th century BCE, those who are balding can now take comfort from considering heaps of sand.

Eubulides, a pupil of a pupil of Socrates, is best known for his many paradoxes, by which he intended to set people thinking. In what is known as his Sorites paradox (from the Greek word meaning 'heaped up'), he poses the question of how we can logically justify applying the term 'heap' to a pile of pebbles or – since you are metaphorically (if not literally) on a beach – sand. Eubulides also produced a parallel argument, known as the Phalakros paradox, about going bald, but more of that in a moment.

Pile up a heap of sand or, if you have a small bucket to hand, make yourself a sand castle. If asked why you are doing such a childish thing, just answer that you are a philosopher! Now there is no doubt that what you have before you is a 'heap'. Thousands of grains piled up in one place deserve, without possibility of contradiction, to be termed a heap. Take one grain away and it remains a heap; take another, then another. At what point do you consider that your heap of sand is no longer a heap? Would three grains constitute a heap? Would a single grain?

Of course one might aspire with William Blake to gain some vision of the world in a single grain of sand. But, mystics aside, one grain definitely does not seem to me to qualify as a heap. But at what point did the heap stop being the heap? And how do you define what constitutes a 'heap' without allowing extreme conditions when commonsense tells us the term should not apply?

And here we can start to move out from what sounds a very narrow question to explore its implications. People have a strong urge to define – to say that one thing is good and another bad, that something is a success or a failure. They define themselves and others by general terms, which is inevitable, for without such general terms how else would we be able to say anything? We need words, and words are general, not specific. We put the individual thing we have before us into a category – and the more categories we have, the more clearly the object is categorized and the better we describe it.

But here's where the Sorites paradox comes into play. In the real world, there are no clear-cut categories. Between success and failure, good and bad, there are a million gradations. To start to define – this is a heap, that is not – is already to violate the particularity of that pile, heap, castle (help, I'm using general words again!) of sand.

People tend to prefer clear, unqualified descriptions, and are often frustrated by those who describe themselves as 'mainly' vegetarian or 'generally' pacifist – but more often than not, in real life as opposed to logic, there is a span of possibilities without any clear defining lines.

People sometimes use an extreme example in order to make a general point. If over-indulgence in alcohol or food is clearly bad, they want to apply curbs to even moderate drinking. Life has to be one thing or the other; you either believe it or you don't.

There is a particular problem with terms that designate a collection. After all, a class of pupils is still a class if one pupil is removed. But can you have a class with a single pupil?

Presumably, yes. But a class with no pupils? Sometimes we can turn such ambiguities to our advantage. If you want to claim that a book you have written is your 'bestseller' you only need to produce two complete failures, and ensure that the third sells a single copy.

So how can all this prevent baldness?

In his Phalakros paradox, Eubulides points out the obvious fact that anyone with a full head of hair cannot be described as bald. Pull out a single hair and the head of hair remains. Pull out another … and so on. At what point do the few remaining hairs constitute 'a head of hair'? At what point does the person become bald? My step-grandson, casually surveying my own shining pate, declared 'Little tiny one!' He had found a hair, so I am no longer bald; or am I?

I may secretly allow a few more hairs to grow. Most will still think me bald; but I may beg to differ.

So a heap or a bald head only becomes one when you choose to call it so. But surely, it's either a heap or not a heap, you are either bald or you have a head of hair, albeit thinning. I'm not deaf, just a bit hard of hearing! He's not effeminate, he's sensitive! She's not overweight, just nicely rounded! But when does the plain person start to be considered beautiful? When does the intelligent youngster become a prodigy?

It's said that nobody aspires to be average. To be average it to fail to qualify for those descriptions we most crave – successful, wealthy, elegant, beautiful. But a moment's thought will show that every one of those descriptions is threatened by the Sorites paradox – success for one is relative failure for another; one person's wealth is another's poverty. When it comes to describing quality and quantity, we either compromise or qualify terms out of existence.

Or you can rebel against ambiguity. There came a point in my own balding process when I could no longer stand a head that resembled a desert criss-crossed with sparse vegetation. I took the 'Nietzschian' option and applied a razor. We force things to be one thing or another.

But definition and the way in which we understand description often lead us astray. You may find that the advertised 'sea view' from your hotel window requires neck-aching contortions, indeed you may find that there is hardly space to perch yourself on your 'balcony' in order to get the advertised sea view. Both balcony and sea view may be correctly so described – after all, you can get out of the door and onto this narrow pelmet of concrete projecting from the sheer face of the hotel wall, so it's a balcony. It is also possible, for those with the head for it, to lean over said balcony and squint in the direction of the sea. Your complaint cannot be upheld – it is indeed a balcony with a sea view, but it is not what you expected. Why? Because we attach to words some ideal meaning, and are frustrated when reality does not match it.

Plato considered the possibility that particular things were no more than images of some ideal 'form'. Every tree is so described because it is an image of the 'form of the tree'. But actually, as biology evolves, we see that it is no longer viable to make absolute categorizations of that sort. All living things are related to one another. One species blends at its extremes into another. We categorize and carve up life and think that we have thereby understood it. In reality, all life is fluid and changing; nothing can be permanently or accurately defined.

Logic and science define and classify – genera, species, classes of things. We set them all out and appreciate their differences. Except that life is never like that. There are no identical human beings, even if all come under that classification. There are no identical, standardized balconies or sea views – every one of them is unique, that's the joy of life, but that's also its frustration.

Should you think such questions trivial, apply the Sorites paradox to the unborn child. At what point does this bundle of cells become a living being? At what point a human individual? Day by day, throughout its time in the womb, the child is changing. Medical science and ethics require that we mark certain significant points along that path towards birth, so that we can justify how we regard the unborn. Is it a human person or is it not?

Of course, if there's money involved, it's wise to call in the lawyers to get everything specified to the point at which any ambiguity can be eliminated or at least made defensible in law. Where there's government involved, the tendency is to specify exactly what is and what is not a failing school or a good hospital. And because what seems like success in one place may be failure in another, there is the tendency to go for evidence and statistics. Everything is measured and evaluated on that basis. And yet, as teachers and medics will be quick to point out, we know the extremes when we see them, but defining the point at which failure grows into success or vice versa cannot be an exact science.

So we have our fundamental question: how do the particulars we encounter relate to our general words? When is a balcony not a balcony? What counts as a genuine sea view? Am I bald or not? And is this a heap of sand?

02

Did you bring your laptop?

What happened to that dream? The laptop was meant to free us from the bondage of the office. The advert promised that we could work from the beach, relaxing by the ocean while earning our fortune with the gentle slithering of finger over touchpad. Given the means to work anywhere, the hard-pressed executive would be able to work from his or her home or holiday home in the most congenial environment, freed from the stress of commuting to the city. But what has actually happened is that work has thereby extended its reach to colonize what used to be vacation.

Recent research shows that up to one third of executives take work with them while on annual leave – or at least check their emails on a daily basis – and many claim that they returned from their holiday feeling more stressed than before they left. Companies give out laptops and smartphones as slaveowners once gave out shackles.

The advert showing the young, informally dressed, highly intelligent, creative, beach-relaxing, laptop-user might have suggested 'You can work *there*.' But it could equally mean 'You can *work* there.' What a difference that change of emphasis makes!

And that difference reflects a more fundamental question: Does your work and its pressures mean that you need and deserve to take a rest from time to time? Or does your work justify your holiday, on the grounds that relaxing and taking a break will serve to improve your performance when you return? If the former, the implication is that you have basic human needs – including the need to be refreshed and not overworked – and it is right that you should take time away from work in order for those needs to be met. If the latter, then the holiday may be primarily justified in terms of work – a brief respite for routine servicing of the machine in order to maintain efficiency.

We are in danger of being trapped. On the one hand we know that relaxation and a generally lowering of stress levels can improve performance. Hence the holiday can be justified as a tool for improved productivity. But once we argue in those terms, then the holiday is hostage to the work fortunes, and if the hoped-for improvement through rest is outweighed by the damage done by absentee executives, then the laptop and Blackberry may threaten to haul them back. But once we allow work to justify rest, we no longer work in order to live, but live in order to work – and that was always the fundamental distinction between the freeman and the slave. Work, for the slave, is an end in itself, not a means to achieve something better – unless, of course, the slave is plotting and planning to earn or snatch his or her freedom. At that point, the slave is already mentally free. The truly enslaved cannot imagine being other than they are.

Anticipation fuels both fear and excitement. Checking work while on holiday can allay the shock of returning to unknown crises. Will I still have a job to go back to? Are there decisions I need to take this week? What if they need me and I'm not available? What – worst of all – if they find they can do perfectly well without me? Engaged, problems require solutions and stimulate adrenalin and action; at a distance, they may stimulate only frustration and helplessness. And it is anticipation that kills present enjoyment. After all, the condemned are hardly likely to relish their final meal, even if the breakfast before the gallows is of their own choosing. Hence the checking of emails and the taking of decisions while away; we do not want to be 'out of the loop' for long enough for our position or authority to be eroded.

Short breaks are the worst. If you want to maximize interest, then the short break offers the most stimulus; after all, if your attention span is limited and you can't relax, you don't really want that second week on the beach. For the first couple of days you remember what you have left behind, guilty about things not done, anxious about those to whom you have delegated responsibility, but by the time that phase has passed, you are within a day or so of re-entering the workplace and the curse of anticipation kicks in. Hence the value of the present moment, and with it the 'beach' opportunity to get a new perspective on one's life, is squeezed into a diminishing time slot. The short break is a stress-inducing period when the problems remain, but one's ability to deal with them is reduced.

How do we cope with that? There are two possibilities:

- The first is to cultivate the ability to live in the present moment (and there are plenty of guides to help you with that, from self-help manuals for the stressed, to meditation techniques). If that is possible, then you become more effective in your use and enjoyment of the present, and that will presumably allow you to relax and prepare to act decisively when you re-engage.
- The second is to use your 'beach' time to reflect on the place and importance of work within your life. For a lucky few, work and life might become one and the same thing, their creative activity so pleasurable, and so central to their lives, that they would want to engage in it all the time and everywhere, rendering holidays unnecessary. But for most, since Adam and Eve were expelled from the Garden of Eden and required to till the land rather than picking the helpfully-provided fruit, work remains a necessary burden. It also remains a way of defining who you are, and when you have either too much of it or too little, it detracts from your self-esteem. Later in this book we shall return to the question of what part work plays, or should play, in your life.

So where does that leave us on the laptop question? Should you take it, or should you deliberately cut off from the world of work? (You can, of course, take your laptop or smartphone for many other purposes – personal communication, searching for suitable places to eat, checking if your flight is going to be delayed, checking the weather. You can even get apps that tell you the time of high tide and the location of the best beach, but for the purposes of this question we'll ignore these bits of added internet value.) Are you going to keep fending off the emails between helping the kids build sandcastles – an activity whose transient results reflect what most of us achieve at work anyway?

Your answer to the laptop question springboards into a whole range of existential questions: What part does work play in my life? How much do I need to control and be in charge of my communications? Do I pretend that I am indispensable? What if I never returned from holiday? What matters most in my life? Where do I most want to be at this moment? What do I most hope for, or most fear? And how many people on this 'beach' with me are free and how many remain slaves?

AT HOME

You might like to read Alain de Botton's *Status Anxiety* (Penguin, 2005) and *The Pleasures and Sorrows of Work* (Penguin, 2010).

You might also look at adverts for laptops and smartphones, and check on the phrases used to encourage people to buy them. What do they say about the potential user? And is that me?

Are you *predictable?*

We like to feel that we are dependable – predictable in terms of our values, dispositions and views – for that is what gives our life a definite character. Without that measure of predictability, relationships as we know them would become impossible. But we don't want to be totally predictable or determined by external forces; we like to retain a semblance of personal choice and creativity. The problem is how we reconcile our experience of personal freedom and limited predictability with our knowledge of how the world works.

We generally assume that nothing happens without a cause, even if, at this moment, we do not know what that cause is. So, to be consistent, we should assume the same of our every thought, word and deed. As we open our mouths to speak, what we are going to say is already part of a causal series. Indeed neuroscience tends to assume (even if it cannot prove) that the process of neurone firing has already determined the thoughts that will give rise to our words and our actions. And that process is assumed to have been initiated by yet another causal series, and that by yet another. Everything that happens at this moment appears to be totally determined by antecedent causes. We cannot escape asking 'Why?', 'Why did I have that particular idea?', 'Where did it come from?' And if a psychologist cannot give us the answer, we assume that some day a neuroscientist will.

Determinism in its most obvious form is exemplified by the French mathematician, astronomer and statistician Laplace (1749–1827), who argued that, with a perfect knowledge of the universe and its laws, the future would be as clearly known as the present, and who, when asked about the place of God within that scheme, famously declared that he had no need of that hypothesis. Nothing would be left to chance; everything would be explained. Of course, the human brain is so complex that, although neuroscience can map out the functions of its different parts, we still do not know exactly why particular neurons fire when they do. It is one thing to *describe* something, quite another to *explain* it. But one day, perhaps we will. Does neuroscience thus make robots of us all?

When determinism was limited to a crude claim that all physical things were linked to one another in causal chains, we could at least assume that, because we know we make a difference, there must be mental input at some point. Hence Descartes, who saw mind and matter as utterly different, struggled to find some point in the physical chain of events to explain how our thinking and willing could make a difference. He mistakenly located that point of mind/matter interaction in the pineal gland – nicely tucked away between the hemispheres of the brain. It was probably not a bad guess, since it is well supplied with neurons yet connected into the body's blood supply, but we now know it generates hormones rather than thoughts.

In a world of scientific analysis and prediction, apparent randomness may suggest a failure to appreciate the complexity of the system, and uniqueness is no more than a single instance of otherwise repeatable and predictable occurrences. And it's really no use citing Heisenberg and his uncertainty principle (that you cannot get an accurate measurement of both the position and the momentum of a particle simultaneously) in order to attempt to find a gap through which freedom might insinuate itself – for that principle applies only to the sub-atomic world, not at the level of our experience.

And the implication of this? There are two ways of looking at the interface you have with your world. Observed, you are part of a conditioned and analysable world; your every action determined, because seeking out causes is what we naturally do to the phenomena of our experience. Indeed, Immanuel Kant argued back in the 18th century that causality was one of the things that our minds impose upon experience. Externally, (in the *phenomenal* world, to use Kant's term) we are conditioned. But as we are in ourselves (the *noumenal* world) we are free. The key question however, is whether – as Kant claimed – we can, at one and the same time, be *phenomenally* conditioned and *noumenally* free. If we are, then perversely, we can enjoy experiencing our own unpredictable freedom while remaining predictable. But are the two really compatible, or is the experience of freedom always an illusion?

That's all part of the matrix of questions explored within The Philosophy of Mind, and fascinating it is. But as we sit on our beach, contemplating the meaning of our life, we should perhaps focus on the more existential aspect of this: Is our own predictability (if demonstrated to our satisfaction) something to be welcomed or feared?

Determinism is uncomfortable. But a milder form of determinism now dominates our lives. We are bombarded with adverts for exactly those products that we are statistically likely to want – based on age, gender, level of income and so on. Our own interests are specially catered for, and thereby often shaped, by those who think us determined by our circumstances; predictable customers. This is irritating, because I like to think that I am free to make my own decisions, and find it frustrating that – more often than not – friends will guess correctly what I am going to do.

Of course, if you allow yourself to become the object of examination, you will indeed be predictable, but that's very different from the way in which you experience yourself. And you are likely to know other people not simply by observing them, but by entering into a relationship with them. There's an element of that in all our experience. I describe things in terms of what they are *for me*, not just what they might be *in themselves*. We can never know anything completely; at some point we have to take a pragmatic decision that we know enough for our purpose. And, of course, what that purpose is will vary with circumstances. The degree to which I need to know someone whom I wish to marry, is rather more than what I need in case of taking him or her on as a new employee within a company. All knowledge is functionally mediated.

So it would seem that imaginatively appreciating another person – the task of biographers – is as valid a way of understanding character as scientific examination. After all, a neuroscientist may describe the brain response to emotional trauma, but it takes a measure of personal empathy to understand the scale of that trauma or its significance for the individual. So where has this got us?

- From your standpoint as observer (especially if aided by Laplace's perfect intelligence), you might argue that all apparently free acts can be explained.
- From your own experience you know what it is to be sufficiently free to be irritated by attempts to predict what you will freely choose to do.
- But the key to our dealings with the world is often functional. My relationship with another person influences how I see them.

So what do relationships tell us about the freedom/predictability question? For a relationship to work, I need predictability. If your responses to me are random, I cannot get to know you as a person. And I assume that you have to deal with me on the same basis, gradually getting to know me through limited prediction. I know what it is to be free. I must therefore acknowledge that (although I cannot experience it) you possess similar freedom. Without that, your response to me would be sadly and totally predictable, and I would be robbed of a genuinely mutual relationship.

Hence, from a functional point of view, we have to assume that determinism is limited – and that includes the sort of determinism that neuroscience aspires to produce. Even if every thought and feeling were precisely correlated with bits of brain activity, I still have to assume that you have a measure of freedom, if I am to engage with you as human to human. If you and I are both totally predictable, our relationship also is predictable, as is my asking if I am free, and my thinking about it, and everything that follows from it. Universal predictability, even if logically possible, makes ordinary life impossible. It may be right that we are theoretically predictable, but we must live as though we are not.

So, do you think of yourself as predictable?

AT HOME

Consider how much you need other people to be predictable, and how much you want them to be free.

04

Back to nature?

Early morning mist hangs over the mudflats, the silence broken only by the calling of wildfowl as the birds move along the edge of the water, feeding, taking to the air, then landing to feed again. I sit contentedly in the hide, binoculars at the ready, waiting. Then I feel a gentle trembling and a moment later I hear it – the unmistakable, bell-like, triple call of the Blackberry. I have an email. I may have come down to the sea again, and sense the running tide, and yet, for me, the wild call that cannot be denied is trumped by another. I reach into my pocket.

But should I? Which should take priority at this moment, nature or my personal network of communications? That may depend, of course, on whether I'm waiting for some vital piece of personal information. But leaving that possibility aside, is there a valid, perhaps an important case for turning the phone off before leaving society in order to commune silently with nature? After all, nature has long been a source of inspiration, whether through the Zen tradition of simple attention to the natural, or the eremitic tradition of western monasticism – seeking solitude in the more remote of places in order to find some 'higher' sense of meaning in life – to say nothing of its contribution in art, poetry and music. So should we turn off the clutter of thought and disengage from literal or imagined conversations when we engage with nature?

Should we turn our backs on society in order to get into it, if only for a short 'beach' spell?

Getting back to nature, of course, is something of a misnomer; we never leave it. We breathe, we eat and drink; our bodies themselves are part of the natural world, with their own little ecosystems. The bacteria in my mouth and gut continue on their natural way whether I am having a day in the office or out here in the wilds. We remain part of nature from birth to death; the process of ageing and the threat of disease are constant reminders that the natural will finally trump our artificially constructed worlds of culture and self-esteem. To die is the most natural thing in the world, however much it may smash its way uninvited into our planned and ordered lives. Taking the healthy lifestyle option, going to the gym regularly, popping rows of supplements at the breakfast table – these may give us the sense that we are in charge of our own personal corner of the natural world, but one day, inevitably, we will be proved wrong.

So how do we get a proper perspective on these two overlapping worlds of nature and culture? Here are some random thoughts:

- Ancient Greek temples display perfect geometric form, imposed on the natural chaos of a rocky hillside, a sign that civilization has planted itself upon the landscape.
- The builders of Stonehenge not only plotted and mapped the movement of the sun, but organized upon the surface of the earth a pattern to reflect their world.
- In the 18th century, formal gardens tamed nature; plants, trees and lawns were strictly ordered and set out. Man, assumed to be the measure of all things, measured and laid out an alternative form of nature, through which one could wander and enjoy beauty without encountering the chaotic or the threatening.
- The Romantics of the 19th century sought to integrate their own emotional lives with the flow of nature; to be wild in a carefully thought-out way; to give a sense of naturalness to a garden, enhancing nature to please

the senses; to build a new ruin, or an appropriately named 'folly' on a manicured hillside or to one side of a lake, in a way that is pleasing to the eye. Nature, it was still assumed, could always be enhanced.

* Just as the old 'Natural Law' approach to ethics did not simply describe how creatures (including humans) behaved in nature, but rather set out to consider how they should behave in a nature *interpreted by reason*, so the formal gardens of the 18th century or the romantic ones of the 19th assumed that nature was just waiting for human interpretation and improvement.
* Bonzai – nature at its most contorted; the result of carefully controlled arboreal torture. Enough said.
* Topiary – don't get me going on that daft, transformational fantasy!

And today, aware of what damage the human species is doing to the rest of the natural world, we use Astroturf to compensate for where nature lacks green, all-weather durability, and take eco holidays to explore the wild in five-star luxury.

The fact that we live simultaneously in the worlds of nature and culture is reflected in our description of people – some are mannered, others natural; some artificial, others genuine; some intellectual, others intuitive. But, like the bonsai, we may feel that our growth has been shaped and contorted to fit a pre-established idea of what we should be. Education – that brilliant method of passing information and life-skills from one generation to the next, without which the whole edifice of cultural life and civilization would have been impossible – is also the tool for easing us from the exclusively natural world of the moment of birth into the world of the mind, culture and society. Civilization is human topiary! OK, so that's all a gross oversimplification and one-sided view of the relationship, but it at least raises the question of how we relate to the natural world.

Yet there is something wonderful about getting back into the natural state. Walking through wild, untamed countryside, sensing its natural acceptance of us but also its threat, we recognize the value of the natural world for itself and not just for what it offers to the human species. The philosopher Peter Singer claims that to privilege the human species above others is 'speciesism', to be rejected along with racism and sexism. Nature should not just be evaluated on a utilitarian basis for what it can offer us – although rainforests may indeed hold secrets for future drugs, and biodiversity may ensure the long-term stability and health of our evolving ecosystem. Humans are a recent arrival on this planet. For millions of years nature was free from human interpretation or interference; in the long-term future, when the human species will have died out, nature will continue, albeit in a form we cannot imagine.

Jean-Jacques Rousseau (1712–78) considered that we are all born into a state of natural goodness, later to be corrupted by the temptations of society. Others, particularly Thomas Hobbes (1588–1679) saw the natural state, with all normal social restraints removed, as one in which life would be, as he famously put it, 'nasty, brutish and short'. Are we innocents corrupted by society, or savages tamed by it? The jury is still out on that one – and so it will always be, since we cannot view ourselves in a totally natural state. We have evolved into social creatures, see everything through that social prism, and cannot pretend to know how we would have been if that had not happened. We can no more know how we would have been without society, than how we would have been if we had not been born. We inhabit the social world and there is no going back; our language, our thoughts, our appreciation of nature itself is steeped in a cultural and intellectual heritage that we cannot shake off.

Nature, of course, is far from benign. When Nietzsche spoke of a return to nature, he indicated that it was more an 'ascent up into the high, free, even terrible Nature and naturalness'. Nature as a whole is indifferent to its various forms of life, its huge vitality destroys that which it produces. It is humankind that seeks to find comfort in a rationalization of nature, an attempt (from the Stoic 'logos' or principle of reason, to the idea of a creator God) to make our place in the world bearable. In fact, nature can be indifferent to us and all else. The universe is not necessarily a comfortable, reasonable place in which to live.

Returning to nature may involve leaving the comfort blanket of control and reason to enter into a zone where creatures eat and are eaten, where they breed and are slaughtered. Of course, as we said at the beginning, we live in that world all the time, it is just that we choose to inhabit that part of the natural world in which reason delivers the good life. We order our steak medium-rare, with a garnish and fries; we do not have to plunge our teeth into a living creature.

So do you really want to enter into raw nature, or would you prefer to see it through rational, moral, purposeful glasses? As soon as we philosophize about nature, we impose our ideas upon it. There are many opportunities within philosophy to explore this – from the Greek distinction between *nomos* and *physis* (order and nature) to Nietzsche's contrast of Apollo and Dionysus, life and nature, and perhaps even to the philosophical and psychological responses to Darwin's theory of natural selection.

Sometimes nature appears to be a threat waiting to be reasoned away, on other occasions it is the source of vitality into which we can plunge – shedding reason as we roll naked in wet grass, run downhill through woodland, or approach the moment of orgasm. We may even temper our plunge with reason, trusting in the parachute, the bungee or the safety harness to protect us as we experience the adrenalin rush.

So, here I am in the hide, knowing – although I cannot see it – that the little red light is flashing in my pocket. Do I reach for the phone? Even if I know that, statistically, it is most likely to be an email trying to sell me something, reminding me that my subscription is due, or that there is a special, internet-only offer available until the end of the month, I still hope that the message may be personal; that someone still wants to contact me; that out here on the mudflats, I am still in touch with the social world. Someone may need me urgently; something may be wrong at work; it may be an old friend wanting to get into contact again. There is comfort in that world, and in the ongoing story that is our life.

But in the moments of solitude, with wind coming off the salt marsh and no sounds but those of the birds, there is a sense of self and of the place of human life in a greater 'scheme of things' – until I catch myself, with that very phrase, trying to avoid uninterpreted nature.

Read *Animal Rights* by Peter Singer if you want to consider our moral response to nature.

Read Rousseau if you're feeling naive; Hobbes if you're feeling cynical or Thoreau's *Walden* if you're seriously into the simple life, or dip into any book on the history of garden design and feel the temptation to improve on nature.

Or just go for John Masefield's poem 'Sea Fever' if you must go down to the sea again, or Wordsworth's 'Tintern Abbey' if you sense his need to reflect on the countryside while 'mid the din of towns and cities'.

05

Does morality add up?

The thoughtful 'weigh things up' to achieve 'a balanced view', but they would probably resent being referred to as 'calculating'. Yet it is remarkable how often we try to decide moral issues on the basis of calculation, weighing the probable results of what we propose to do, hoping that the future will justify our present choice, and that the good results will outweigh the bad.

Developed by Jeremy Bentham (1748–1832) and John Stuart Mill (1806–73), utilitarianism is generally summed up as claiming that the right thing to do is that which seeks 'the greatest good for the greatest number'. This phrase was first introduced by Francis Hutcheson, who used it to evaluate political systems, the best form of government being that which offered the greatest benefit to the greatest number of citizens. It became, and remains, the most popular of all ethical theories. After all, common sense suggests that you judge an action right or wrong according to its intended aim: if good is the intended result, then it's OK. But since we are never certain about long-term consequences, we can at least say that our intention should be to produce, on balance, more good than harm.

Utilitarianism is regarded as the most secular and logical of arguments, in that it does not require belief in absolute moral principles, nor justifies them in terms of God or some overall purpose in life. The right thing to do is to try to achieve some good in the world – seems obvious!

Of course, there are many simple examples to show that adding up expected results does not necessarily give us morally acceptable (or morally inevitable) results. Given the chance of killing one innocent person to save many is the classic example of deciding morality simply on the basis of adding up – whether it's the temptation of the transplant unit who sees the healthy visitor as a potential supplier of any number of desperately needed organs, or the switching of points on the railway to divert a runaway goods vehicle so that it kills one innocent person rather than half a dozen. Reflecting on any of these thought experiments, you know perfectly well that minimizing damage done will still leave you feeling guilty if you are the one to order the death of even a single innocent person. Morality doesn't just add up; it is also to do with our emotional engagements with the world. Some argue, along with David Hume, that we have a natural sense of compassion in the face of suffering, a deep sense of empathy towards our fellow human beings, and this is the starting point both for morality and for the sense of guilt when we sense that we have done wrong, no matter how much the narrowly utilitarian assessors, calculators at the ready, inform us that our choice was the one that minimized suffering.

The most harrowing example of this is found in William Styron's novel *Sophie's Choice*, where the source of a young woman's overwhelming sense of guilt is revealed in the terrible choice she was forced to make in a concentration camp – choose which of your two young children you wish to save, or both will be killed! She chose, saving one life, and suffered the emotional consequences. Would it have been easier to have allowed both to die than to choose between them?

One of the most commonly rehearsed criticisms of utilitarianism is that we never, finally know the outcome of our actions. At its most crude, one argues that the small child saved from drowning (an archetypal 'good' action if there ever was one) may grow up to be a serial killer. One could ask if it would have been morally right to strangle Hitler at birth. But, of course, one would not have known then of the future career of dear little Adolf, so the action would clearly have been judged wrong. But with hindsight? Weighing it all up?

But what if our efforts achieve nothing? At the end of his *Methods of Ethics* (1874) Henry Sidgwick wrote (in a passage cut from later editions) that, if the visible world is the only reality, then morality is 'reduced to chaos'. He clearly thought that, if death were the last word, there would be no final result to justify morality. His morality was held hostage to the one thing he most craved but could never know, and he spent many years searching for proof of life after death.

Life is short and uncertain; we suffer its accidents randomly; disease kills good and bad alike. We make our choices, but nothing is guaranteed; we assess benefits, but nothing is certain. But we can at least try to take everyone's preferences into account and hope for a final balance in favour of the good. That surely is the morally responsible thing to do, a process that nobody would wish to challenge.

Yet here is Sidgwick, shoving a philosophical spanner in the works. If there is no life after death, he argues, morality is thrown into chaos. The implication of this would seem to be that, for morality, adding up is not enough; we also need to believe that, in the end, it will also have something to contribute that is of lasting value.

But does it? Clearly, if one accepts that death is the end of life, the final reckoning is always going to be zero. Good or bad, all end up dead, their balances cleared. Vanity of vanities, all is vanity; the universe finally freezes; there is no end result that makes any sense to us. In the absence of some sense of on-going or ultimate value, utilitarian calculations are suspended over a void. If they are ever going to 'add up' we need to have some sense that there are objective moral values independent of immediate results.

That does not mean that utilitarianism is not valuable. In the ordinary course of things we always act according to our expected results – that's how human beings have always operated. Indeed, you could argue that intelligent life has developed primarily in terms of getting results – our senses enable us to relate to our environment, find food, mate and defend ourselves. All sentient creatures seek their own 'good' in one form or other; it is the most natural thing in the world. Utilitarianism adds value to that natural process, by arguing that the potential benefits and preferences of everyone involved should be taken into account. As a short-term strategy, it works well. Choose values for the here and now; decide what you stand for, even though you will not stand for long.

When the Earth is no more and the universe returns to the pure energy whence it came, ashes to ashes, even the finest religious, cultural or moral artefacts will have come to nothing. In utilitarian terms, they will fail to 'add up' to anything. Is that cynical nihilism taken to the final degree? Or is it the liberating recognition that there cannot be a final account, that nothing is guaranteed, and that our choices are ours to make and to live with? Whichever view you take, one thing cannot be avoided: if utilitarianism doesn't 'add up', the very fact of our experience of moral choice – our sense that there are some things that we 'ought' or 'ought not' to do – implies that, at some level, we believe that there are objective moral values, even if they cannot be justified rationally.

AT HOME

Read J. S. Mill *Utilitarianism* for the classic work on this theory.

Most introductions to ethics have a chapter on utilitarianism – see, for example, *Understand Ethics* in the Teach Yourself series.

For the most harrowing choice, read *Sophie's Choice* by William Styron.

06

Should you regret being prudent?

A few years ago there was an advert for a popular brand of vodka, which showed a line of camels heading off into the desert, their riders – so the image implied – imbued with the spirit of adventure, eagerly anticipating the unspecified challenges of dangers that lay beyond the distant horizon. The caption read something like 'I used to take the caravan to Clacton until I discovered ...'. We smile, and suddenly that very sensible holiday we've planned seems something of an embarrassment; we've settled for less than our inner hero deserves. Those who become mildly inebriated (on vodka or anything else) sometimes sense that there is more to their life than prudence would dictate. Those who, with genuine or 'Dutch' courage (another use of the word 'Dutch' that rightly infuriates the good citizens of the Netherlands, since there is certainly nothing bogus or phoney about the Dutch) head out into the desert, may die in the process; those who settle for the domestic caravan site will suffer no such risks. So should we regret being prudent?

Prudence implies cautiousness in practical affairs – to be sensible and morally aware, concerned with providing for oneself and others, thoughtful about the results of actions. By and large we approve of the prudent as they take reasonable steps to provide for their own needs; they resist becoming a burden on society.

Aristotle considered that reason allowed a person to seek their chosen end or purpose, and to evaluate practical actions and decisions that allowed that purpose to be fulfilled. This he termed *phronesis*, which is generally translated as 'prudence'. As he explains in Book 3 of his *Ethics*, the temperate or prudent person is moderate in enjoyment of pleasures and not distressed when they are not available. The ideal life is one that embodies a rational and balanced approach, achieving *eudaimonia*, living well and doing well. The prudent strike a mean between timidity and rashness, and thereby fulfil their own nature as part of a rationally ordered world. What more could one want?

But into this neat rational approach to life there comes a fissure, sides of which were represented in Ancient Greece by the Stoics, who saw the whole world as a rationally ordered place, and the Epicureans who considered the world to be mechanistic and impersonal, and who therefore considered that humankind should be free to set its own goals and enjoy such pleasures as were available. For centuries, influenced by Western religion, the majority view was to see the universe as rationally ordered, and prudence as the way to achieve fulfilment, whether in this world or the next. But with the rise of modern science in the 17th and 18th centuries, the shift went towards the Epicurean side – with the world seen as an impersonal mechanism, within which we should set our own agendas and seek our own fulfilments. But in such a world, prudence may not always feel like the only sensible option; natural selection, after all, favours those who thrive and breed, not necessarily those who are cautious.

To risk everything on the throw of a dice; to take a leap of faith; to commit to a relationship without having been given cast-iron guarantees that it will bring happiness; to believe in order to understand; to go beyond the call of duty; to step beyond the dictates of reason – is this a better policy in a world without guarantees? The choice is everything, so if you're into angst-ridden but challenging Danish philosophy, try reading Kierkegaard. But the real challenge to prudence comes from another 19th-century philosopher – Nietzsche.

> '... the secret of harvesting from existence the greatest fruitfulness and greatest enjoyment is – to live dangerously.'
>
> Nietzsche *The Gay Science*, 1882, Section 283.

Nietzsche saw moral rules and regulations as guard rails to prevent people falling over a precipice, a safety net for life. But those who dare do not need such a net. The risk of the fall is part of the enjoyment of walking the precipitous path. He advocated living dangerously; saying 'Yes!' to life in spite of its limitations! To take the Nietzschian option is to be bold, to grasp opportunities whenever they present themselves. In popular culture it is to march forward singing some combination of '*Non, je ne regrette rien*' and 'I did it my way.' Chance never favours the timid. Except, of course, where the bold are unthinkingly heading over a cliff, while the timid slow to a halt and peer over at the doom they have just avoided; guard rails, even if despised by Nietzsche, can have their uses.

A common view of philosophy – especially of the professional sort, slicing and dicing arguments and making subtle distinctions – is that it is a safe but boring activity, a predictable and precise option for the career academic. It must rate highly, along with librarianship, the museum service and the Inland Revenue, on the list of preferred occupations for those who like to see life well-ordered, rational and easily justified – although, on second thoughts, perhaps the Inland Revenue should be removed from that list. But this view arises largely because philosophy comes in two very different flavours.

In science, according to Thomas Kuhn, there are long periods during which normal science follows the parameters of an existing paradigm, or established way of understanding things, interspersed with periods of dramatic change during which a new paradigm emerges to replace the old – as happened when Einstein burst out of the structure of

Newtonian physics, or Darwin's theory of natural selection gave impetus to evolution rather than fixed design as a way of understanding living things. The same happens in philosophy. Great thinkers produce insights that can totally change the way we see things, but they are followed by intellectual acolytes who develop and refine their work. Sticking within an established philosophical paradigm, theirs is a safe, prudent place to be.

But great thinkers take intellectual risks. Take Wittgenstein. His early work inspired and encouraged the Logical Positivists and others to judge all statements meaningful in so far as they conformed to experience. But then, by the time his paradigm was becoming established within the academic community, he returned with a philosophy that was entirely different. Gone was the requirement that meaning went hand-in-hand with evidence; now meaning was related to use. Language was a 'form of life', a 'game' with its own rules; instead of trying to analyse it and justify its claims, he encouraged the philosopher to observe how language was used. And by the 1950s, just as his new paradigm was becoming enshrined within the English-speaking philosophical world, only his early death prevented him from launching out into yet another approach – the quest for the foundations, or unquestionable assumptions of our thinking. That is the boldness of a great mind – to create, rather than follow intellectual fashion.

By contrast, the goal of the paradigm-following professional philosopher is the waspish tweet, the article in a peer-reviewed journal that demolishes a tiny but essential bit of argument. Swords come out, and thinkers defend their intellectual corners. But more often than not they fight in confined spaces, using very similar weapons, and it is sometimes difficult to distinguish victor from vanquished.

But the Nietzsches or Wittgensteins of this world, be they philosophical, scientific, religious or literary, plough a lone furrow. They live dangerously; think thoughts that are radical and untested, look at life in ways the implications of which they have yet to measure. Copernicus, priest and astronomer, would have slept more easily had he stuck to the traditional view that the sun revolved around the earth. He had no proof that it was otherwise, and was still committed to traditional ideas of the perfection of circular motion in the heavens, but he published his radical heliocentric thoughts anyway, with an introduction claiming that his ideas were simply a means to simplify astronomical calculations, rather than an attempt to describe reality itself. In effect, he was saying 'We know, for good religious reasons, that the sun goes round the earth; but wouldn't it simplify our calculations if we could think of it as the other way round?' – now that was a prudent move! Galileo argued that Copernicus had correctly described reality, and paid the price for doing so.

But for most, whether philosophers or sane, the crucial questions are not so much intellectual as personal. Did you have the courage of your convictions? Did you compromise? Did you go for that opportunity when it presented itself? Of course, following Aristotle's advice, it is wise not to go to the other extreme and be rash. Gamblers seldom win long-term. But timidly following the paradigm – whether that is intellectual, social or even the paradigm set by a family, imposing values from generation to generation – is seldom going to lead to a life of human flourishing.

And if you were to find yourself near death and reflecting back on your life, what would you most regret? The moments of foolish chance or the moments of prudence? Would the sensible thing seem more a lack of courage? A failure of nerve? Timidity? Lost opportunities? Would you want to be thought of as someone who always played it safe?

Perhaps being away from your home environment, seeing new people, new places, gives you a chance to be more adventurous and risk-taking than otherwise. A holiday may be just that time to live dangerously – dipping a toe in the water of risk, knowing that the familiar will return in due course. But when you return home after your break away, will you hope to be more prudent or to be less?

AT HOME

Read Aristotle's *Ethics* and/or Nietzsche's *Thus Spake Zarathustra or Beyond Good and Evil* or Kierkegaard's *Either/Or.* If packing your caravan for a local destination, you might even like to consider a nip of vodka!

07

Is the universe meaningless?

If you're reading this book sequentially, as opposed to dipping into it (although there's nothing wrong with that, of course, beaches encourage dipping), you may still be pondering whether or not you should be prudent, and where you stand on that question will, in part, depend on whether you see the universe as a rationally ordered place, or an impersonal environment within which you can be free to set your own agenda. So let's stand back and look at that broader question.

Something is meaningful if there is a context within which it makes sense. Words have meaning in the context of language. Ask for the meaning of any word, and you get an answer that relates it to other words. Ask for the meaning or significance of some instrument or dial, and it will be explained in terms of the machine that it is monitoring. Ask about the meaning of a piece of legislation, and it is related to the society upon which it is imposed. 'What's the meaning of this?' asks the outraged schoolteacher, suddenly coming across pupils misbehaving. It's no use arguing that the behaviour has no meaning. What the teacher wants to know is how that particular behaviour relates to how one is expected to behave. In other words, we generally speak about things being meaningful if we can relate them to an overall sense of purpose, or direction, and that requires seeing not just the thing itself, but its context.

My life might be given meaning in terms of my family and friends, my work, the place where I live, the circles of those who share my interests or religious beliefs. Human life as a whole might find its meaning in terms of its place in the biosphere; Homo sapiens appears to have quite an exalted (although not permanent) place within the tree of life. But life itself? How do we justify or find a context for this thin film of green and blue over the rocky ball that is the Earth? It is, after all, a very temporary phenomenon, lost within a universe in which matter is the exception and empty void the norm.

Is there a purpose behind these expanding galaxies? What was the purpose of the Big Bang? Can gravity act for a purpose? Is there any meaning or purpose displayed in the fact that the Andromeda galaxy, being rather larger than our own, will soon (in cosmic time) come to dance with it, swirling together and reforming our world? We will, of course, long since have ceased to exist, both as a species and as a planet. Then, we shall have ceased to exist even as a separate galaxy.

Nietzsche argues that the universe cannot be considered a machine, for that requires purpose, nor can it be either noble or heatless, for that is to anthropomorphize it. Yet we're still tempted to see it as a machine, simply because it feels more comfortable to do so. And faced with suffering, or the immensity of space, or the frailty of humanity, or the overwhelming power of nature to destroy, we are tempted to say that the world is pitiless, that it is heartless. Even Marx, in his critique of religion, described it as the heart of the heartless world – it was the effort of humankind to give meaning, and find love, where there was none. He saw it as a delusion, albeit a powerful one and one that answered a universal human longing.

The question we can't answer is whether or not the universe itself has any meaning. And we can't answer that because it would require us to step *outside* the universe in order to see it in context. That we cannot do.

So the ultimate dilemma is this: Everything has its meaning given in terms of its context; but 'the whole' has no context, therefore it can have no meaning.

That does not imply that we can prove that the universe has no meaning in any absolute sense – for to do that one would need to see it in context (which we can't do) and show that it was not connected with its context. It simply means that there is no way of knowing whether the whole has meaning or not. The most fundamental question of all, therefore, has no answer.

But even if we despair of *finding* meaning, that still leaves open the possibility of *creating* meaning in a way that enables us to find satisfaction, perhaps even comfort. But how can we do that while retaining intellectual honesty?

Just as Immanuel Kant (1724–1804) argued that ideas of space, time and causality were *imposed on* experience by the mind, as a necessary way of making sense of things, but did not reflect the way things were *in themselves*, so we may find ourselves coming to the conclusion that the quest for meaning in life is just a natural feature of the way human minds work. There can be no 'objective' proof of meaning, because meaning is not part of the external, objective world. Rather, meaning is a feature of how we engage with the world and deal with it. And it seems to be a necessary way for most people, without which we may lapse beyond cynicism into existential despair.

We know what it is to do things purposefully; we search for food and drink, for a mate, for shelter against the elements. We take an 'intentional' stance towards the world from the moment we are born. The world is not some external structure, it is something of which we are a hungry and thirsty part. Even at the most basic level our activity is purposeful, and that purpose is related to a wider context – our own survival. Creatures adapt to their environment if they wish to survive. Those that do not adapt are culled by the process of natural selection.

So meaning and purpose are basic features of the way in which we live. We are not spectators but participants! We rebel against meaninglessness, because we live by meaning and purpose; we live intentionally. Meaning is not an added extra to something I find in the world; meaning is the relationship I have with the other pieces of the world that I encounter. In other words, even if – from an impossibly 'objective' point of view – I might declare the world 'meaningless' on the grounds that it has no detectable context, from a practical and personal point of view, I operate on the basis of meaning and purpose.

That is not to anthropomorphize the world. The virus that attacks me has no overall place in the scheme of things other than to thrive and flourish as a virus, just as I seek to thrive and flourish as a human being. There is no 'personal' approach to the turning of galaxies, and we cannot expect the universe as a whole to pay any special attention to our own planet, or species. But the question of whether it is therefore meaningless, although logical, is actually rather fruitless. We have already seen that there can be no logical answer to it, since we cannot see the universe as a whole in context, but the mistake was to ask such a personal question of something we have attempted to explore in a detached and 'objective' way.

How you choose to see the universe is how you choose to see the universe. Anthropomorphized, it is a pretty heartless, cruel place. But should we try to anthropomorphize it in the first place? The world as we encounter it is shot through with meaning, value, purpose, beauty and awe-inspiring power. None of that is the result of a physical calculation; none of that exists in a world that is considered only from an objective point of view.

In the end, it comes down to a commitment to engage with the world, rather than to take a detached view. Do we shrug our shoulders, admit that we cannot prove that the universe has 'meaning', and just carry on living? The detached view, which is not a natural one for human beings but has to be learned, sees the universe as meaningless; the more natural, engaged encounter fills the world with meaning. Does that make meaning self-generated? Of course, but it is none the worse for that. Giving the world meaning is a profoundly human activity, manifested in religion, philosophy, literature, philosophy and all the arts. It is also expressed in the drive to understand that characterizes the sciences. Is that invalidated by the simple fact that we cannot get outside the universe to contemplate its context?

So – as you sit on your beach contemplating the meaning of your own life – do you consider the universe as a whole to be meaningless?

AT HOME

As in all the best self-help approaches to life, start with a list of those things that give your life 'meaning'. To what extent is the meaning of each of them given, and to what extent is it self-generated? If they were removed from your life, would you still think of yourself has having meaning? Other than Prozac, is there any answer to a feeling of meaninglessness?

Would you take a holiday from paradise?

Paradise was established in the second millennium BCE, in neolithic Persia. And the reason for that is quite simple: track the word 'paradise' back through Latin and Hebrew to the ancient Persian, and you find that, quite simply, it is the term for an enclosure. But probe a little deeper and that enclosure becomes of the utmost significance for the development of humankind.

Take your flocks grazing over wild terrain and you become aware of your vulnerability – you are a tiny outpost of human society in the midst of an inhospitable and uncaring nature. The sun becomes too hot or the water too scarce and you perish. But create an enclosure where you can stockade your animals and meet with other people, where you dig a well for water and start to plant crops, and you get the sense that life is more predictable and orderly. Animals can be counted and traded, wealth and social position established. You have tamed a corner of nature; you have established a zone that is designed for human benefit; you have created the first paradise. Villages, towns, cities – all spring from that basic enclosure. Think Las Vegas in the midst of the Nevada desert – and, yes, I admit that some of us might prefer to take our chances with the desert!

But paradise, as a place for human comfort and provision, became more than a city. It morphed into the idea of taking nature and perfecting it through the application of human reason. The garden, our next form of paradise, shapes nature for our delight, a place of refreshment, gentle on the eyes, harmonious to the senses.

Thus paradise is the image of the world as we might have devised it for our own benefit. And if that is not how we see our present world, we project it back into the past (a Garden of Eden from which we were expelled) or the future (as a heaven in which we hope to awake after the sleep of death). The dead are 'called home' to a paradise, after their labours on Earth.

But we can get hints of paradise here and now. The holiday paradise is where you go to be pampered. And paradise lurks in the advertisements for the new development of luxury apartments; a paradise of smiling friends having meals together and admiring one another's furnishings and spacious accommodation. Or for the more senior, it is the paradise of silvered and distinguished age, solidly healthy and comfortable, enjoying the well-deserved benefits of capital accrued through the years of working, the couple smiling and waving off their visiting offspring, content to live in their retirement paradise. Just take out the additional pension and all can be yours!

Of course, not all human developments are enhancement of the wild state; most are ugly, rectangular wounds, where vegetation surrenders to concrete. So there emerges another form of paradise – the unspoiled wilderness, of beauty as yet unsullied. But this, of course, is something of a misnomer. Unspoiled wildernesses are fine, provided they are visitor-friendly. An unspoiled wilderness in its raw state is likely to spell death to the unprepared human. The wild is paradise only to those with romantic notions.

Manicured, ordered and safe, the paradise garden is contrasted with the inhospitable wilderness beyond its bounds.

But Genesis suggests that Adam and Eve are not satisfied with their nursery world; their enlightenment in the form of knowledge of good and evil leads to their expulsion. They are cast out into the world where they will only survive through work, labouring to till the land, rather than grazing on ripened fruit. Paradise comes at a price; it is not for those who ask too many questions.

So how long would you remain in Adam and Eve's garden? If everything were provided for your comfort, your every physical and material need met, would you want to remain immobile in that place for ever? Is the new apartment or retirement home a place from which you would never feel the need to wander?

The Buddha considered a life devoted to the needs of the senses to be that fit only for grazing animals, which fits his own experience, having been brought up in luxury, shielded from the harsh facts of life and death, until he chose to leave his paradise in order to seek enlightenment.

Campers regularly leave centrally heated homes, with running water and sanitation, electricity and gas, refrigerators, televisions and all the other trimmings of life, to go and pitch a tent. From the paradise perspective that seems madness. People choose to put themselves through some discomfort to explore somewhere new. They climb mountains for no purpose other than having done so; they cycle across countries and run marathons without having been forced to do so, and with perfectly useful vehicles available for covering the same distance with minimum effort.

So even if everything imaginable were provided in your domestic paradise, you might still want to take a holiday from it. The same people who are offered the luxury apartment are also targeted by travel companies for the most exotic of holidays.

Aristotle argued that women and slaves were not able to organize their lives effectively – slaves because they lacked ability, women because they lacked emotional detachment. It was in their interests, therefore, to organize life for them – to lay everything on, to create an appropriate paradise. Even in more recent attempts to establish a planned economy that would usher in the dictatorship of the proletariat, there were many attempts to provide all the material goods and services that were seen as the basis of the good life, and the lure of every sect is to offer paradise in return for absolute loyalty. Offer up your freedom and autonomy, and we promise you a world in which everything is provided! You are relieved of existential doubt and the dilemmas of the marketplace; you simply follow instructions. But beware attempting to eat of the tree of the knowledge of good and evil.

And curiously, that is still the mantra of much modern politics – the economy is key, life for each generation is expected to be better than that enjoyed by the last. Paradise forever deferred. And was Jerusalem builded here, among these dark, satanic mills? All utopias are forms of institutional paradise. There is an old saying that it's better to travel hopefully than to arrive. Perhaps that applies to paradise. To seek something better gives motivation; to settle for what one has, with all energy expended on defending and protecting, leads to social paranoia and stagnation.

So are your holidays simply an opportunity to enter a paradise in which you can be pampered, tucked up and taken care of? Or do you intend to peep over the walls of your enclosure and try something new? In fact, given the chance, would you take a holiday from paradise?

09

Is moral relativism absolute?

When it comes to morality, it's all too convenient to make an absolute distinction between:

- Relativists – who hold that there is no objective basis for morality, but that it is a human construct, based on values and traditions that are passed down within each particular society and culture.
- Absolutists – who argue that morality is (or should be) based on pure reason, on some feature of human nature, or on rules handed down by God.

To the relativist, the absolutist is old-fashioned, inflexible, and wedded to an outdated view of God, the universe and everything. To the absolutist, the relativist threatens all the values that make life worthwhile. But it's not quite that simple.

For one thing, absolutists would argue that, even if moral principles are logically or factually established, it is always important to take particular circumstances into account. Thus the absolute rule that it is wrong to kill may be modified in cases of self-defence, or in order to permit killing if its intention is to prevent the slaughter of innocent people. It is also notable and those who argue most vociferously for absolute moral principles may also support the death penalty for murder, allowing that the killing of a killer does not go against the principle that one should not kill.

But that said, there seems something rather egocentric about willing that one's own moral principle should become a universal law, which is what Kant proposed. True, it may give logical validity to one's own conviction, but it may not go far in persuading someone whose moral instincts are radically different. All actions are unique; we distort and limit them if we try to make them fit rules, or judge them according to universal principles. So should we veer back towards a more relativist position?

The relativist equally modifies the 'anything goes' caricature with which the absolutist might wish to identify him or her. Even if there are no objective criteria for deciding matters of right or wrong, moral discussions and progress are still possible, on the basis that morality is closely related to the fundamental values that are inculcated during childhood and which may serve as a basis for social cohesion. When ethical push comes to philosophical shove, the relativist is likely to start talking about adopting policies that lead to human flourishing or the overall wellbeing of society. But that is not too far removed from the old Natural Law or Virtue Ethics approaches, which sought to justify moral claims in terms of a reasonable interpretation of human nature or the virtues required for human life to fulfil its potential.

But moral relativism, in its desire to allow that everyone should be free to develop his or her own moral position, argues that it is wrong to impose absolute rules. This is based, of course, on a fundamental value – the autonomy of the human individual. So just as the tolerant person will tolerate everything except intolerance, so the relativist will take into account a wide range of moral positions provided, of course, that they do not claim to be absolute. And that, of course, appears to be the one absolute rule of every relativist. I may disagree with what you want to do, but I defend your right to want to do it. On the other hand, if what you want to do is destructive of human society, then I will exercise my right to oppose it in order to defend society. Through this kind of argument, the relativist tends to make morality the means to a social end.

So relativism is not entirely divorced from factual considerations – indeed, if it were, there would be little scope for discussion, progress, or moral sensitivity. If morality is the product of history or biology, the moral sceptic will still consider that some choices are better than others, and will see the value of morality as a tool for social improvement. This is clearly evident in Mackie's *Ethics: Inventing Right and Wrong*, 1977, which is still a wonderfully clear presentation of the issue.

Of course, the simplest way to check the presuppositions of any ethical argument is to adopt the infuriating position of a five-year-old: just keep asking 'Why?'. If they remain sane and good tempered, the person you question in this way will eventually be forced to reveal them.

There are many reasons for claiming some form of absolutism, if only to probe the basis for ethics in the first place. Thus, for example, Thomas Hobbes argued that people needed to band together and agree the principles of social order in order to establish security, on the ground that nobody wants to live in constant fear. This gives at least some basic assumption – what it means to live the good life, the nature of human flourishing – that can be accepted as a desirable end point, which can then determine the nature of moral claims. But that still depends on your view of society. It could be argued, for example, that competition and war helps society to grow stronger and evolve. What then of a morality that promotes peace and harmony?

But for absolute certainty in moral matters, we have to assume that there is some ideal, neutral viewpoint to which everyone would agree, were they not prejudiced by their particular circumstances. The problem is that there is no such complete objectivity, no 'view from nowhere' that can be used as an unquestioned and universal point of reference.

So we are into an interesting dilemma:

* Press the relativist and eventually you will come to some implied value (Human flourishing? Human autonomy?) that underpins moral claims and thereby serves as an absolute point of reference. As we suggested above, the absolute for most relativists is relativism itself.
* But press the moral absolutist and you find a relativist lurking, willing to modify or qualify his or her principles in exceptional circumstances, recognizing that you cannot get an absolutely neutral standpoint, nor an individual action that exactly fits a universal category.

This touches on a fundamental aspect of human experience and thought; we experience particulars but think generalities. The particulars throw up variety but our mental tendency is to find some overall narrative that will accommodate that variety. To get away from particular rules and regulations, we aspire to the freedom of individuals as an overarching principle. But it is just as 'absolute' as any other principle, even if flexible in its application.

You can *explain* differences – after all, we are all subject to influences in our upbringing and environments – but that does not necessarily *justify* differences, or provide a way of adjudicating between them. To understand all may be to forgive all, but that does not deny that there may be something that needs to be forgiven. In other words, beneath every socially sensitive relativist there may lurk a more fundamental and absolute moralist fearful to get out.

But that is not to introduce some overall metaphysical principle to establish morality; it is simply to point out that we all acquire sets of principles by which to live, and these (whatever their origin) seem to us to be objective. They are used to make moral choices and judgements, and appear to be self-justifying, in the sense that they are, for us, the starting point and not the conclusion of a logical moral argument.

But there remains a logical flaw with a strictly relativist position. Relativism is ultimately self-defeating. In order to doubt or criticize anything, you need a point of view, a position from which to get a perspective on the options as they circle around you. Perhaps that ultimate, fixed point is simply the conviction that everyone is entitled to do what seems best in the light of their own cultural situation. But why should that be so? Why not accept intolerance as one more valid option? Whether or not it is ever articulated, or even acknowledged, every relativist has some particular view, some unchallenged assumption upon which everything else is based; it could not be otherwise. Without some foundational value, relativism should logically lapse into silence; the silence of weightless freefall, where there is no gravity to determine up or down, and where there is nothing to be said about right or wrong.

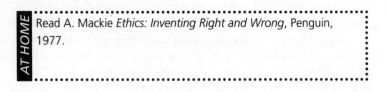

AT HOME

Read A. Mackie *Ethics: Inventing Right and Wrong*, Penguin, 1977.

10

Putting down roots?

There are at least four types of holidaymaker:

* The explorers – out to see something new and wondering at strangeness; they wander as far as they can afford and are always tempted to go native on food, drink, music or whatever. Fundamentally, they are pioneers with ABTA-bonded safety nets.
* The hedonist-invalids – out to get a bit of rest and recreation to recover from the stresses of work, possibly requiring a little cultural input, but mainly there to enjoy the rest. Cruise liners are full of them, especially those who are on the permanent vacation to recover from a lifetime's work. The younger variety reverse the process, embarking on holiday with an agenda of pure hedonism, but often ending up the worse for wear.
* The merchant adventurers – out to plunder for souvenirs and experiences to share with friends back home. On holiday, they become extended outposts of their social network, scouting in order to report back.
* The colonizers – whom we shall consider here.

You don't have to lie dead on a battlefield far from home to claim that there is a corner of some foreign field that is forever England, or even like the poet Rupert Brooke himself – in a curious irony, given that 'The Soldier' is probably his best-known poem – to die abroad and be buried in an olive grove on the island of Skiathos, for there are a substantial minority of holidaymakers who choose to colonize.

The cicadas may be strumming away outside, or new fragrances floating on the warm evening air, but the internet radio is tuned to Radio 4, providing the shipping forecast and the Archers as audible background for drinks on the terrace. There is something reassuring about having the control of an environment that familiarity brings, and for the most determined colonizers the whole domestic package, suitably scaled to fit, can be exported. Caravans and motorhomes spread out from their island base, some flying the Union Jack. Cars speed towards familiar holiday homes, hauling boxes of Earl Grey to territories where the only known form of English tea comes in Liptons bags (and rather good it is, too, should you venture to try it!). Such colonizers cannot comfortably stir far into the unknown without taking with them some tokens of their identity.

More common is the desire to colonize in the sense of putting down new roots in a holiday destination. There is the advantage of already knowing that friendly baker on the corner who starts producing baguettes at some ungodly hour, or noticing familiar faces; you are greeted in the street and take delight in being known. You are part of this place, even if you visit it only once or twice a year.

Do I belong 'here' or 'at home'? Indeed, is this my real 'home'? It's all too easy to get a superficial sense of belonging, generally based on relationships that are, in essence, commercial. The local traders know and welcome us. But they would, wouldn't they! How deep are these roots? Is the cemetery full of our ancestors? Is this the language in which we habitually think?

Notice that there are two very different processes going on here:

* The exporters of identity take tokens of home with them; wherever they are, they are outposts. While we recreate the familiar, we can hold on to what we cherish wherever we are. Standards are maintained as a sign of identity – as happened throughout the British Empire in the 19th century. It was seen as exporting civilization; in reality it was the attempt to maintain identity in far-flung places.
* Others seek to put down new roots in the culture in which they find themselves. They immerse themselves in their new environment and borrow identity from it. Soon, returning again and again to the same 'beach' they will think of it as 'home from home'. They build up a set of memories associated with this place, and thus allow it to become part of their own story, their own identity.

The second of these processes reproduces our earlier development as individuals. We become who we are because of all that surrounds us, we experience it and take it into ourselves. That sense of self gives a comforting illusion of permanence. Even as we travel abroad we can say 'See, I am in a new environment and yet still very much myself!' To explore somewhere new might just give the possibility of imaginatively entering into a new life. What would it be like to live here, to be from here? I could have been different. That very possibility may be experienced as threatening – the recognition that everything about me is a product of chance and circumstance. It is natural for our emotions to reject such radical contingency and hold on to the familiar. Travel in New Zealand and you're bound to come across someone from Surrey or Hertfordshire – and what a comfortable feeling that brings!

And here our travel habits reflect the most obvious general difference between plants and animals; the former put down roots, fixing themselves to the spot from which they hope to receive nourishment, the latter go hunting for food. And, of course, it is this feature of animal life that requires us to have senses. Without senses and memory we would soon die, either from starvation or by becoming food. We would certainly fail to develop kinship bonds or social life. Faced with a threat, we run away, or prepare to fight. If the environment is harsh, we travel on hopefully. We nourish ourselves from what we find when we explore our environment; as happens in the first moments of life, when the baby searches its new world for the nipple. Previously fed by the root of an umbilical cord, in an enclosed womb; now, out in the world, it is programmed to start foraging for food.

Plants aren't like that. They are fixed and await their fate. In need of sustenance, they simply put down deeper roots. If the roots fail, they die. Many plants can suffer huge damage and yet, with roots intact, start to grow again, and grasses, as gardeners know to their cost, simply go on growing from the ground up the more we mow them down.

Curiously, our colonizing holidaymakers are reverting to plant forms of emotional nourishment; either by taking roots with them, waiting to plant them in some corner of that foreign field, or by seeking soil into which to set an entirely new rootstock.

Push the analogy a bit further, and we start to see many features of human life that are plant-like. Some people seem to cling to the most unpromising territory, with roots that somehow seem to nourish them on the most inhospitable rocky cliffs. Although we have the physical ability to adapt ourselves to very different environments, try new forms of food, travel and communicate as never before, in our emotional lives we may still feel the pull of the older plant-based way of life, or clustering together, putting down roots, seeking reassurance about who we are and where we belong.

It is literature rather than philosophy that has explored this phenomenon; from the excitement or trauma of leaving home, to the vision of life as a quest, or the feeling that 'back home' there is a reliable, steady and accepting environment to which, in our more nostalgic moments, we long to return.

The whole process of growing up is a movement from a womb/umbilical cord model, to one where we are off looking for a breast; testing the boundaries of the familiar, venturing forth and then retreating until confidence builds.

So in the process of reflecting on who we are and what we are looking for in life, conducted in the moment of 'beach' relaxation, it might be as well to consider where we stand in the spectrum of emotionally charged behaviour that goes from the exporting of roots on the one side to the desire to lose oneself in new experiences on the other. Holidaymakers heading down that motorway are either plants or animals in their intentions.

So, looking around you, are you planning to put down roots, or taste and move on?

AT HOME

Read Rupert Brooke's *The Soldier*.

Get any magazine on buying property abroad and speculate on what you would be feeling if you bought a holiday home, or perhaps moved abroad. What image would you have of yourself there?

11

High enough for Nietzsche?

Lace up your boots; plan the route; look up towards the snowline and feel the challenge. In an hour or two you're going to get an entirely new perspective on this place, tucked comfortably in its valley; you are going to climb.

And running though your head is *An Alpine Symphony* by Richard Strauss, weaving its tapestry of sound as it depicts walkers moving off at dawn to climb through forests and past streams, until the sun rises over open alpine pasture in a glow of expansiveness. The burst of sound as you gain Strauss's imagined heights gives you a tingle. That symphony does for mountains what Vaughan Williams' *Symphonia Antarctica* does for icebergs and glaciers – the sense of wonder at their raw expanse and power; the fragility of a human individual set within the majesty of nature; the music hitting you like the slap of icy wind.

People have elevated thoughts, adopt a superior attitude, look down on others. They try to get an overview, or see beyond or above their immediate problems. They may be invited to up their game, or to aspire to higher things. Gaining height may be a challenge, but not always a comfortable or socially acceptable one.

It was certainly never seen as a comfortable option for Nietzsche. At the opening of his strange, quasi-autobiographical proclamation *Ecce Homo*, he describes philosophy as 'a voluntary living in ice and high mountains – a seeking after everything strange and questionable in existence, all that has hitherto been excommunicated by morality'. It is wandering in what he describes as the 'forbidden', as ascending to a place that is inherently dangerous, a place where error is rooted in cowardice and truth is something that one has to dare; a place, in other words, where one can set aside all conventions and think the unthinkable. True philosophy is about exploring a new and higher perspective, freed from the limited conventions of the comfortable lowlands. Nietzsche – in one of his megalomaniac outbursts that colour *Ecce Homo* – claims that his *Thus Spake Zarathustra*, is not only 'the most exalted book that exists' but that it is 'the actual book of the air of the heights'.

OK, so as I slide my rucksack off my back and collapse down on the grass after a long climb, I prepare to luxuriate in the elevated view. Out on this hillside, life is clean, simple, a matter of breathing in the fresh air and feeling the warmth of the sun. This, it seems, is so much better, more elevated, than the routine of office politics, or retail complaints, of professional rivalries or domestic drudgery. Down in the valley people appear no more than tiny dots going about their business. This is, in part, why we have hiked up here into these wild open spaces. It's not just the need to get out into nature (we've considered that already) but also the need to get this dramatically revised perspective.

One of the key features of philosophy is that it tries to get a view of each problem from an elevated position. Where the easy option is just to be immersed in the everyday problems and issues, the philosophical option is to stand back and consider the overall patterns that define life, the values expressed in it, and the direction it is taking.

At the beginning of *Thus Spake Zarathustra*, Nietzsche describes the prophet coming down from his mountain fastness after a long retreat from human society, and being amazed to find that people do not know that God is dead. As

Nietzsche observed a fundamental shift in the beliefs and aspirations of mid-19th-century Europe, he is amazed that most people cannot see what is happening all around them. The gods of the old order are becoming powerless, people have taken a sponge to wipe away the familiar horizon of their world, it is becoming colder as the untethered world drifts through space. And he sees clearly that something new is needed to replace the old, vanished certainties. Let the *Übermensch* arise; let us make him the meaning of the earth; man is a creature waiting to be surpassed. Philosopher as prophet; philosopher as seer; philosopher as offering a higher perspective. Whether you agree with Nietzsche or not is hardly the point. What he presents is the challenge of looking down from a height that makes most people dizzy; to peer unflinching over the precipice without the comforting security of the old guard rails of conventional morality and habitual thought. Do you dare to think like this? To question everything?

And if you want to sit down, out of breath, after a few hundred yards, do not despair. In *Human, All too Human*, Nietzsche claimed that, in the mountains of truth, one never climbs in vain. Either you get higher today, or you exercise your strength so that you can climb higher tomorrow. Just keep at it!

Of course, the tracks above the intellectual snowline are fraught with dangers. If you are a professional philosopher with a career to consider, best hone your arguments into journal articles that will position you strategically within the web of your peers, satisfy the needs of the Universities Research Assessment, and thereby secure additional funding for your department. Take the safe option. Don't even think about trying to follow Nietzsche's example if you fear being misunderstood.

But there will always be those who, risking academic respectability and the mockery of their peers, want to climb up whatever tracks the logic of their thoughts takes them. So, as you lace up your philosophical boots, ask yourself 'Am I prepared to risk going high enough for Nietzsche?'

AT HOME

Decide for yourself whether *Ecce Homo* (trans.: Hollingdale, Penguin Classics, 1979) is a sign of Nietzsche's coming madness, or the bravest possible statement about his philosophical aspiration. But if you are unfamiliar with Nietzsche, please read *Thus Spake Zarathustra* first!

12

Is your thinking engaged?

The most interesting and challenging thing about philosophy is the way in which it can engage with life, challenging our comfortable assumptions and inviting us to look again at what we have previously taken for granted. That is why Socrates is a philosophical hero – not necessarily because we agree with his views (or at least the views that Plato ascribes to him in his dialogues), but because he is the archetypal intellectual nuisance, the person who asks the uncomfortable questions and presses arguments until their concealed nonsense is revealed.

At its best, philosophy, like religion, impacts on every aspect of the life of the person who engages with it. That is one of the things that distinguishes philosophy from science. The latter (if we discount the subjective inputs that can creep into science, or the personal attachment that scientists can have to their particular theories) aims to provide a disengaged and objective analysis of information. It may require serious personal commitment and benefit from intuitive mental leaps, but at the end of the day, the scientist wants to set out theories that are supported by evidence, bracketing out his or her personal preferences.

Of course, science was originally called 'natural philosophy' and there has always been an overlap between the science and philosophy, with that latter often taking on the task of exploring the general principles, presuppositions and context of the former. Science and philosophy have also been allies in the task of sorting out whether it is reasonable to believe factual claims. So, for example, when it comes to sorting out sense from nonsense, it is useful to stab any claim with David Hume's 'fork'. In assessing metaphysics and claims about divinity, he argued that one should ask whether it contains:

- experimental reasoning concerning matters of fact
- abstract reasoning concerning quantity and number.

And if it contains neither of these, it should be rejected as 'nothing but sophistry and illusion'. Hume's view reflected the science of his day, which claimed to have banished superstition in favour of reason and evidence.

Now, when it comes to judging metaphysical claims that may have been fair enough. But in the more personal, existential aspects of life, it has never been that simple. Hume's idea of morality, for example, is based on the belief that everyone can be altruistic and feel a natural sense of compassion when confronted with human suffering. But that is not necessarily provable by observation (there is always going to be evidence pointing to natural selfishness and indifference) nor is it a matter of logic. So it would be wrong to assume that Hume wanted to banish everything other than analysis and logic from our thinking.

Although Hume argued that we could not show that causation was other than a habit of mind (having seen one thing follow another repeatedly, I assume that the first is the cause of the second), he recognized that the idea of causation is an important factor in our psychological development. In other words, the engaged business of dealing with life will require things that our rational mind is not (yet?) able to justify.

There is a difference in scholarly opinion as to whether Hume was arguing that causal powers did not exist, or simply that, even though they do exist, we cannot have direct knowledge of them. The latter has always seemed to me the more reasonable interpretation, since Hume was concerned to show the limitations of what we can know. You can't get far unless you accept causality and the regularity of physical processes, even if it would be sophistry to claim to have certainty about either of them.

Therefore it is important to recognize an element of existential application in all philosophy. Not necessarily Sartre's existentialism, with its challenge to strive for personal authenticity and take responsibility for shaping our life, but in a broader context. The wisdom that philosophy seeks is not just cleverness, it is also insight; cleverness may get neat answers, but insight shows relevance.

To think clearly and to analyse data – that is a valid function of philosophy, and one that brings it close to natural philosophy (science). But philosophy is also engaged with questions about the meaning and purpose of life, what the 'good life' should be, and moral issues that follow from it. It is as much involved with values as with facts and, at its best, it should always be ready to show its relevance and defend itself against the 'So what?' question of the cynic, while at the same time asking 'So what?' of all other claims – teasing out their significance.

In the context of Eastern thought, there is little distinction made between philosophy and religion. Take early Buddhism. Since it does not require belief in a god or gods, it can (from a Western perspective) be described as a philosophy or ethical system. But that is not adequate – for Buddhism has many elements of worship and meditation that are also clearly what in the West we would see as religion. But those things aim at leading the Buddhist practitioner to deepen his or her emotional engagement, which then allows the intellectual perception of the nature of reality to take on personal significance. It is one thing to accept that 'all compound things are subject to change' or 'there is no fixed self' as intellectual ideas, quite another to 'see' them as living realities, which is what Buddhist philosophy invites you to do. In other words, what Buddhism implicitly recognizes is that assertions about the nature of life, however useful, are not enough; you need personal engagement to back up intellectual assent.

Take the idea of evolution on the basis of natural selection. Once it is perceived as a hypothesis, one starts to see the world differently. The issue is not just the truth or otherwise of the theory (and all theories, if genuinely scientific, are open to be challenged) but its impact on our self-understanding. Hence much of the controversy surrounding Darwin, both in the 19th and 20th centuries and continuing into the 21st, is not about the brilliantly simple and (with hindsight) obvious arguments that build up so impressively in *The Origin of Species*, but the way natural selection totally changes the perceived relationship between humankind and other species. All life forms are seen as related, as part of a single process of evolution. Humankind has no special place in the scheme of things, but is the product of a most awesome process over even more awesome periods of time. It opens up self-understanding and insight in a way that can be threatening to those schooled in more traditional, homocentric approaches.

From Wittgenstein's idea that the meaning of a word is to be seen in its use, to Heidegger's consideration of the way in which things are encountered as tools to be used, philosophy has recognized that our practical engagement with life can provide the starting point for our thinking. And that's not so very different from Socrates, who challenged, questioned and examined the very things most people took for granted. But the importance of that approach is that it forces us to pay attention to the implications of what we habitually do or say.

So, as we unroll our towel on the philosophical beach and prepare to reflect on life, we should remember that philosophy is not simply a matter of engaging in conceptual Sidoku, making ideas fit together into neat patterns. The key thing is to understand how our ideas impact on our lives, to evaluate them on that basis, and – where possible – to act upon them. Only then does philosophy get engaged and come alive.

Hume's 'fork' is found in his *Enquiry Concerning Human Understanding*, section XII, Part III, or just search for it on the internet for a summary and comments.

Or, to see engaged philosophy at work, just dip into one of Plato's dialogues, or perhaps try Sartre's *Existentialism is a Humanism*.

13

Would you still bet on God?

At first glance, Pascal's wager seems one of the saddest arguments in the Philosophy of Religion. Blaise Pascal (1623–62) was a brilliant mathematician and physicist who, in the last eight years of his life, devoted himself to philosophy and theology. In his *Pensées*, he looks at the options and decides that it is worth betting on belief in God.

He starts from the position that we cannot know whether God exists or not. That being the case, is it still worth believing in him? He considers the possible outcomes of believing or not believing and presents his argument along these lines:

* If you believe in God and he exists, you are likely to gain an infinite reward.
* If you believe in God and he does not exist, you have lost nothing apart from the slight inconvenience of being religious, performing rituals and so on.
* If you do not believe in God and he does exist, then you risk eternal punishment in hell and you lose the possibility of infinite happiness.
* If you do not believe in God and he does not exist, you have neither lost nor gained – except possibly the benefit of avoiding having to be religious.

What Pascal has created here is a decision matrix. Through it he suggests that, on balance, believing in God is the best bet. Potentially, you have much to gain and little to lose, whereas by not believing you risk much, with little to gain. And that bet holds whether or not God actually exists.

This argument is sad, from a religious point of view, in that it makes three assumptions:

1   That religion is basically an inconvenience, with little to offer to make it an attractive proposition in itself.
2   That God punishes and rewards according to a person's beliefs.
3   That God can be fooled by insincere belief based entirely on self-interest.

But is this decision matrix still valid? Is there any logical or practical justification for taking a bet on God in the 21st century?

In recent years, and particularly in the light of the resurgent atheist criticism voiced by Richard Dawkins, Sam Harris and others, the balance of probabilities in Pascal's wager has shifted.

1   New atheists would argue that God is not simply an unknowable with a 50/50 probability of existing. They see belief in God as illogical, and his existence as unlikely as it is possible for anything to be.
2   They also argue that religion, far from a mild inconvenience, is positively harmful.

So the matrix becomes:

- If you believe in God, his unlikely existence makes your chances of being rewarded in heaven negligible, so you have little to gain. An infinitely unlikely infinite reward cancels itself out.
- But if you believe in God and he does not exist, not only do you gain no reward, but your life is harmed by the effects of religion.
- If you do not believe in God, his unlikely existence makes your eternal punishment a negligible possibility. An infinitely unlikely infinite punishment is worth risking.

* If you do not believe, and God indeed does not exist, then you are free from religion and superstition, which is a benefit in itself.

On balance therefore, an atheist revision of Pascal's wager is unsurprisingly loaded against seeing belief in God as a good bet.

But the curious thing is that religion continues both to survive and to thrive. It has not withered and died in the face of scientific advance and the logic of atheist criticism. So what is it that shifts the matrix, suggesting that God is still a good bet?

There are two factors that need to be taken into consideration, which do not feature much in the writings of the new atheists:

* There is a tendency for the new atheists to see 'real' believers as those who accept a crude, literal idea of God – as a being who exists somewhere in the universe and is not above the punitive torture of those who fail to accept or obey him. But such belief is no more than a caricature of what belief in God is about for the more sophisticated believer. Belief in a god who exists physically 'out there' somewhere is idolatry. As the theologian Paul Tillich put it, 'God' is the word we use for Being Itself (reality itself, if you like), not the name of 'a being'. So language about God is not about something that might or might not exist, but a way of talking about the meaning and purpose of life. Dawkins and others dismiss such sophisticated belief as a distraction from, or cover for, the naive view of God that they oppose. But that is the equivalent of saying that some crude notion that 'we are all descended from apes' is what belief in evolution is 'really' about, and that a sophisticated analysis of the workings of natural selection and the genetic relationship between species is simply a smokescreen! I know a good number of people who would say that they believe in God, but on questioning them, the God they believe in is certainly not the bogus physical being existing 'out there' in the universe, against which the new atheists campaign.

- The other major factor to be taken into account is the benefit that comes from the whole cultural and social matrix that religion offers – whether it is a sense of the transcendent and inspiration in music, art or architecture, or the personal sense of wellbeing that comes from taking part in life-affirming rituals, or belonging to a supportive community. Many people would have good reason to remain religious, even if it were proved to them that God did not exist.

So let's factor these things into our decision matrix:

- If you believe that God exists in a crude, literal sense, you will be convinced of eternal rewards, and – in the unlikely event that such a god existed – you would receive them.
- If you believe in God in a literal sense and he does not exist, you will never live to find out that you are not to receive an infinite reward after death, so you lose nothing.
- In either case, you may find religion brings personal and social benefits here and now. These options would account, in part, for the rise of religious fundamentalism.
- If you believe that 'God' is a word we use to describe the ultimate nature of reality, encountered personally, the issue of whether God 'exists' or not is irrelevant. Whatever benefit you gain from that option (or disadvantage you suffer) is derived entirely from the implications of seeing the world in such personal, meaningful terms, rather than simply at the impersonal level of scientific investigation.
- If you do not believe that God exists in any literal sense, you have two choices:
  1 To call yourself an atheist, rejecting religion and promoting enlightenment man, with the benefits that come from intellectual integrity and so on.
  2 To call yourself a believer, but accept a non-literal form of God. That way you may accept the benefits of religion, but avoid the atheist criticisms.

But, to be consistent, if you take the atheist option you will need to find some other way of expressing the inspiration that comes from much religious art, the sense of wonder, the conviction that certain values are not merely a matter of personal choice but are deeply engrained in the fabric and nature of the universe.

You may also take what we may call the 'Buddhist option', namely to follow a religion that does not require belief in God. Some atheists dismiss this option, arguing that Buddhism is a philosophy and ethical system rather than a religion, so it doesn't count. But that will not do, and reflects a narrowly Western approach to religion and philosophy. From an Eastern perspective, following a philosophy and living it out through rituals and ethics is exactly what appears to the westerner as a religion.

So where does that leave the modern form of Pascal's wager?

In a literal sense, the bet on some quasi-physical God 'existing' has reduced almost to zero. Our view of the universe and our recognition of the limitations and nature of human cognition make the existence (or our knowledge of the existence) of such a God quite impossible.

On the other hand, Pascal's bet was a matter of looking at self-interest. One might ask therefore what elements in your life may benefit from religion. If there are benefits to be had from a view that the world is, overall, an integrated place with values that are universal and so on, and that through personal rituals you can enhance the sense you have of yourself, and your place within the community – then the option for belief in God may appear attractive.

The worrying aspect of this is the increase in the literalist, fundamentalist wing of religion – a phenomenon which plays right into the hands of militant atheism by its refusal to engage in serious discussion, and which can lead to radical political action, even terrorism, on the back of the absolute conviction about the will of a vengeful God.

Overall, Pascal's wager has become more complex now – the bets are more evenly spread, and the options are far from clear. While fundamentalist atheism and fundamentalist religion attempt to batter one another, many believers, agnostics and atheists continue to enjoy the basic human sense of transcendence and wonder without feeling the need to weigh up the respective benefits in order, consciously, to place their bets on the existence of God.

But we need to remember that the happiness or benefit gained by belief in God does not depend on that belief being true, merely on it being effective emotionally and practically.

I reckon the wager also rather misses the point. My guess is that few people today regard belief in God as an insurance policy against eternal damnation, while many apparently sane and intellectually able people continue to practise religion. The fundamental question we should be asking therefore is this:

- What is the question to which religion is the answer?

In other words: what is it about human life that leads people to be religious? What needs does it address? And supplementary questions to this would be:

- What other answers are given to that question?
- Are those other answers compatible with the religious one?

And, of course, religion remains a phenomenon in most societies, and – like all phenomena – it is open to investigation. The sad fact is that, when those who oppose religion attack only the literal acceptance of the idea that God exists, they do not thereby *explain* anything. All they succeed in demonstrating is that this powerful (for good or ill) phenomenon called religion is not vulnerable to such rational criticisms. Its power lies elsewhere, not in the literal acceptance of apparently incredible beliefs, but in offering a story about the world within which one's life can make sense, or a set of images that give coherence to one's highest aspirations.

So would you still bet on God?

AT HOME

Read *Pensées* by Pascal and *The God Delusion* by Richard Dawkins. Consider the former's view of religion, and whether the latter has actually engaged with the phenomenon of religious belief and why it persists.

14

Were you ever 'at home'?

Your travels over and reunited with your suitcase, you pass through customs and a few minutes later (with luck) find yourself reaching in your pocket for the car keys. The engine sounds curiously familiar and you notice the sweet wrappers on the floor that you'd meant to clear up before you left. The same old traffic. You turn into your road, and a hand is raised to you in friendly recognition; you are back. Your neighbour has changed his car since you've been away, otherwise all seems familiar but enhanced. You start to spot small differences, or things not noticed before. The window frames still need painting, and – after two weeks of neglect – the grass needs cutting. On the threshold is a pile of post. Here we are – home. Your mind is still half on holiday; but you are back in a place that is even more familiar now than it was before you left. What we see everyday fades back into wallpaper; only the unusual commands our attention. But on returning from a time away, the familiar edges into sharper focus.

Sometimes I despair of philosophy, for its rational arguments scarcely do justice to the more subtle nuances of human experience. More can be revealed in poetry, as when in the wonderful final section of 'Little Gidding', the fourth of T. S. Eliot's *Four Quartets*, he says that 'the end of all our exploring' is to arrive back at where we started and 'to know the place for the first time'. And as we reach home through an 'unknown, remembered gate', perhaps not returning from a brief 'beach' visit here, but the return to a childhood home and memories, Eliot quotes from Lady Julian of Norwich, a 15th-century English mystic, that 'all shall be well, all manner thing shall be well'. And that reaching back to a fixed point, where the fragility of the world rests in something comfortably permanent, echoes the mystic's vision of everything that is made being as small as a hazelnut in her hand, and marvelling that something so insubstantial does not simply vanish.

And this sense of being 'home' relates to the idea of the personal *axis mundi*, the centre of our world, which gives meaning to all that surrounds it, defining what is 'home' or 'far away'. So what does it mean to be 'at home'? Why do some see 'homelessness' or 'rootlessness' as a curse while others seek to lose themselves in the anonymity of the crowd, or take to the road in order to find themselves? Culture is full of travels and journeys and returnings, from 'country roads, take me home' or 'by the time I get to Phoenix' to the nostaligic yearnings of 'Strawberry Fair' for she who 'once was a true love of mine'. Or from the Beatles' 'she's leaving' for the girl finally escaping the confines of home, to the curse of the Flying Dutchman, forever sailing his ghostly ship into the opening bars of Wagner's opera.

One thing is certain; whereas for science, space and time are homogenous (even if warped by gravity), for humans they take on emotional qualities, and provide a framework for understanding who we are. The journey of discovery and the returning home are features of our emotional engagement with life, and whether we long for the open road, or are content to remain at home, says much about how we perceive ourselves, and where we find comfort.

But these days, the idea of having a 'home' that somehow defines who we are has become problematic. We move regularly, have friends all over, commute a distance to work, where we meet up with other circles of friends or at least acquaintances. Some people are accused of being more 'at home' in the office than in their own home. Some use work or hobbies to escape a home that does not provide them with a suitable axis to express their life. Some just have a low boredom threshold when it comes to places to live. Some see themselves as genuinely cosmopolitan; if a better job is offered in Hong Kong, they'll go – and, after all, they expect to meet up with circles of like-minded people when they get there, and they can always return regularly to visit friends and relatives. It's a small world; you can live all over! The attraction of cosmopolitanism can be the obverse of the refusal to be given a label. Diogenes of Sinope (404–323 BCE), the Cynic best known for living in a barrel with provocative disregard for any convention, refused to say to which polis he belonged and declared himself to be a citizen of the world, or 'cosmopolitan'.

In some places we feel 'at home', while others strike us as alien, however beautiful. Why then do some places feel naturally comfortable for us? Have you ever come across somewhere in your travels and felt 'I could settle here for life'? Have you found yourself in an environment – perhaps a very pleasant and comfortable one – and yet felt it to be an alien place and yourself lost, or at most passing through, far from home. We instinctively know what it is to be a foreigner or to be at home. It is a sense that this place, these people, know who I am and allow me to be who I am. Here I don't have to pretend. Here I have not just a role to play, but a right to play that role. Here I am ... 'at home'.

What constitutes 'home'? And more particularly, if you have moved around a fair bit in your life: Were you ever 'at home'? In other words, is there some place – from your childhood perhaps, or a significantly good time in your life – that is special for you? If there was one place you would really want to be able to return to over and over again, where would that be?

I want to suggest that being 'at home' relates closely to the way we habitually experience things around us. Our senses place them on a kind of grid within space and time – not just a grid indicating distance or duration, but one that is also an indicator of value and meaning. We create a map around us all the time, a map upon which we chart all that makes us who we are. Our family and friends may be on that map – some close and perhaps dominating our whole view of life, others more distant – but so might our work, our social contacts, our hobbies, our dreams and aspirations. We know where we are at any one time by reference to a number of fixed points from our past or in our present: points of value; points of happiness; points of fear or of desolation from which we want to escape. We carry with us a kind of mental map of what has made us who we are, and we project it scaled 1:1 over the world of our present experience, giving it colour and significance. And so, as we reflect on our life so far, we look back and mentally enter into the maps that we constructed in each of the phases of life through which we have passed. Childhood, school, college, marriage; each will bring into our mind an image, positive or negative, that shows how that time and place has contributed to who we are.

So, thinking back, was there ever a time when you were utterly 'at home'? And, if there was, what was it about that place or that time that gave you that homely feeling? Are those values still with you, or have they been lost along the way? And are they recoverable? 'I was never happier than when ...' says a great deal about a person.

If we were separable from our world, if we were some non-physical thinking entity freed from the constraints of time and space (and Descartes' idea of the self as a purely thinking being might tempt us to take that view) then we might well be able to plan out and establish our ideal environment. We would simply program in what we want from life and, as on the search facility on an estate agent's website, we'd come up with our ideal home. But the truth is that we are not separate from our world. We know who we are only through a natural interaction with what is around us. And if we are to reflect on our own meaning and values, we need to get a sense of where we feel 'at home' – for that is the natural sense of our own localized integrity.

Philosophy will generally encourage you to think and argue about values, personal as well as general. But thinking can get us only so far; there are levels of fundamental meaning and commitment that seem to drive and shape our thinking. We think on the basis of what we feel. And the sense of who we are, given particularly in the sense of where we are 'at home', is as good a way as any to reflect upon the fundamental values and passions that drive us. So were you ever 'at home'?

AT HOME

Read T. S. Eliot's 'Little Gidding' or – for philosophy with a sense of journey and place – Pirsig's *Zen and the Art of Motorcycle Maintenance*.

Consider the fascination people find in exploring English country houses, or ask yourself whether you would consider retiring abroad and, if so, whether you would join an expat community, or go native.

For more on the idea of mapping out your life, see my book *Me* (Acumen, 2009), but read question 35, 'How did you become who you are?' first.

15

Why is consciousness a problem?

Sometimes the most obvious thing is the most difficult to understand. We all know what it is to be conscious, and we can generally tell whether other people are conscious or not by whether they respond to the world around them. We also have no problem ascribing consciousness to an animal but not to a rock. So how can consciousness be an on-going problem for philosophy?

Many philosophers defer to neuroscientists when it comes to the origins of consciousness, and the general assumption within the neuroscientific community is that consciousness is the result of brain activity. Of course, neuroscientists would not claim that our thoughts and feelings are *experienced* as brain activity, simply that they are its product. Francis Crick and others have argued that we are nothing but the action of neurons, and that, if we want to understand consciousness, we have to look at areas within the cerebral cortex.

But consciousness is not the same thing as brain processes, even if it is dependent upon them, and the argument that we are simply the product of neural activity is reductive – a bit like saying a painting is just a mass of drops of pigment, true but inadequate for the purposes of understanding a work of art, although less so perhaps for Seurat, who does wonderful things with dots! When I experience something as 'red' I do not claim that there is some little red image in my brain, but neither am I happy simply to identify the experience I have with the measurable neural activity. I know that my experience takes place at the same time as that brain activity, and appreciate that, without a functioning brain, I could not be having that experience. But that is not to say that the two things are identical. Nor, if the pattern of activity in my brain could be reproduced artificially, would I consider that the reproduced version was exactly the same as my experience of a red object – not least because experience assumes that we experience *something*, a reality distinct from ourselves, whereas brain activity is merely an internal operation.

Some well-known philosophers working in this area suggest that psychology will eventually be replaced by more specific descriptions of brain activity. Paul Churchland argues that a brain state and an experience are the same thing, but we know about them in different ways. I may experience a blurring of my vision when I try to read something close up; the optician measures my eyes and concludes that I need glasses. The measurement and my experience reflect the same phenomenon, but they are known in quite different ways. I experience a headache, you can check to see if the cause is sinister, or merely the result of stress, tiredness or alcohol. 'I have a headache' and 'I am dehydrated' may amount to the same thing, but only the first is known directly, while the second (even if known with reference to past experience) can be measured.

If consciousness and mental activity are no more than the product of brain activity, one implication would be that, if fitted with a suitable readout device, we could detect brain activity a fraction of a second before a conscious decision is made. But that, as we saw when asking 'Are you predictable?' has drastic implications both for freedom and moral responsibility. Whatever brain activity is related to our thoughts and actions, our experience requires us to take ownership of them. Yet, for many neuroscientists, consciousness is an epiphenomenon – a spin-off or by-product of neural activity. If they are right, it is an illusion to think that, by thought or choice, we can change anything. Everything is controlled by our brains; we can monitor what is going on in our cranium, but we cannot influence it. The implication is that it is my brain that does the choosing; to think that the choice is *mine* is an illusion. It seems to me that such a conclusion must be wrong; the problem is seeing how to *prove* that it is wrong.

That's why there's a problem with consciousness. And it's a crucially important problem to solve, for if a narrowly neural view of the self is accepted universally, the implications for how we treat ourselves and others may well be catastrophic. In a world where people are no more than neural machines, they may well be treated like machines rather than unique persons.

It seems to me that consciousness is better explored through literature than neuroscience. It is about relationships, feelings, intentions, fears, ambitions. The fact that each of these things has a corresponding profile in terms of brain activity is about as relevant as the description of a football match entirely in terms of the movement of muscles – it may be true, but it does not convey the significance of the action on the pitch. What we say about brains is not the same as what we say about people. Craftiness or laziness may be features of an individual, but make no sense as ways of describing the activity going on inside his or her cranium. Neuroscience may give a comprehensive account of what happens in the brain, but a psychologist explores behaviour and feelings in relation to experiences and ideas, often relating back to childhood. The one deals with grey matter, the other with relationships and experiences – very different kinds of data for science to process.

But the problem is that, taking the view that everything is physical and that there cannot be a separate non-physical 'mental' world (as Descartes claimed), had led some philosophers (e.g. Daniel Dennett) to deny the existence of experience, a view described by Galen Strawson as incredible. How can you deny what we all know all the time, and which forms the basis of our whole relationship with the world? What Strawson opposes (as do I) is the idea that all characteristics of experience can be described by neurophysiology.

One could argue that the mind is somehow an emergent property of matter. In other words, once matter is organized in a certain way, something else (mind) emerges from it. But the strange thing here is that you have brains that operate, but do not themselves experience anything, and arising from them is a new level of existence, consciousness, which does the experiencing. But in that case, why not simply say that some stuff (in the form of brains and sense organs) can experience? This would suggest that mental reality is a property of physical nature, and hence that there could be a mental element latent within even the simplest of things.

Consciousness is a function. When we say that someone is unconscious, we mean that they no longer relate to the world around them. When consciousness returns, their sense organs start functioning – gathering information about the external world, and they respond, with eye movements, words and so on. We know that they are aware of their surroundings and are responding to them – that's what consciousness is about, not the ability of neurons to fire, but the ability of the whole organism to exercise its senses, collate the information they provide and respond to it.

Without doubt, the head is the part of the body within which we generally experience ourselves as conscious individuals – it is the location of our eyes and ears on the head that starts to give us the perspective and orientation we need, along with our sense of taste and smell. Decapitation is the most effective severing of life; but to locate the self in the head is not the same as saying that the self is identified with the brain. Nor could a brain function – even if it were kept alive – if separated from the rest of the body, at least not in a way that we would recognize as human. It is the whole self that is conscious, the brain merely processes stimuli from the senses and the rest of the body, alongside its more general task of maintaining the body's systems.

You do not discover that someone is a teacher by examining their brain, you watch them at work in front of a class of students. Being a teacher is a social role, it makes no sense to be a teacher in isolation; to teach you need students. So, if one's self-aware mind is to involve all that is key to identity – work, family, friendships, views, preferences – it cannot even be located exclusively within the individual body; the self inhales and exhales, sharing its breath with the world. If our mental life finds expression in relationships, where are they located physically? Where is a friendship? It is real – we all know and experience friendship – but is it located in one or other brain, or in both, or in some strange physical connection between them? Is it located elsewhere? A phenomenon as real as friendship does not have a physical location. Brain analysis of one or other partner in that friendship will not reveal it.

And what kind of process is 'making up your mind'? Can you think of yourself as a neural process observing what you observe and deciding what you decide? The attempt to observe ourselves in that way creates the most horrendous, brain-hurting feedback loop.

And why the insistence that I am something 'more than' what biology and neuroscience can reveal? Because, as conscious centres, we 'have' a world to inhabit. We shut our eyes and it appears to disappear. We dream, creating our own imagined worlds, we have ideas and hopes that transcend what we experience. Hence the belief that this thinking, willing, imagining, creative self is something other than the physical body and brain that are its vehicle in life. But how does that work? How does the basis of what we all experience from the moment of birth relate to our body and its brain? How does being 'me' relate to the me that you can examine? That, in the end, is why consciousness remains a problem.

AT HOME

For a basic introduction to issues in the Philosophy of Mind, try my *Understand The Philosophy of Mind* (Hodder, Teach Yourself, 2012).

Julian Baggini's *The Ego Trip* (Granta, 2011), although mainly concerned with the question of personal identity, provides a readable introduction to some of these issues.

If you're up for a serious challenge, read *Consciousness and its Place in Nature* (ed. Anthony Freeman, Imprint Academic, 2006), in which a paper by Galen Strawson is followed by a set of responses.

Consider whether you can see your eye in the act of seeing, and therefore whether the act of seeing has any place within the world as you experience it.

Or simply Google 'consciousness' and let your mind reel!

16

Successful? Ambitious?

Whenever I contemplate the meaning of success, I am haunted by a brief monologue at the beginning of the film *Annie Hall*, when Woody Allen reflects on the famous comment by Marx – Groucho, of course, not Karl – that he did not care to join any club that would have him as a member. Life, so the Allen character would have us believe, is basically terrible and all too short. These self-contradictory ideas seem as good a place as any to start our quest to understand success.

We have a notion of what success could be, without which we could have no sense of failure. Without a goal we could never fall short; without hope there is no disappointment. So, even at moments when we despair and feel that life is a failure, we must have some idea of what success could mean for us. Woody Allen and Groucho Marx are, after all, hugely successful at presenting an image of what it is not to be successful.

But as soon as we take the step towards defining success, we hit problems. After all, we all wind up dead; so – if judged in terms of an end product – all life ends in failure. Unless, of course, you argue that after death we are rewarded or punished and therefore that we will be recognized as a success even if, in worldly terms, our life has appeared a failure. It was just such a religious hope for compensation beyond the grave that Marx – Karl this time, of course, not Groucho – criticized as deflecting our attention away from the genuine task of improving our conditions in this life, famously describing religion as 'the opium of the people', an understandable drug with which to escape from the constant awareness of present conditions on earth into the dream of heaven.

If you accept the idea of a heavenly reward for the troubles you've seen, even if 'nobody knows but Jesus', then that alone will give you an entirely new criterion of success – you will be judged according to the principles of your religion, quite apart from any earthly success or failure. Indeed, those who suffer martyrdom are the most highly rewarded; the ultimate failure becomes the ultimate success.

However, if you hold no such belief, the task is to try to assess what constitutes success. Aristotle, as the basis for his Natural Law approach to ethics, considered that goodness was a reflection of how well something fulfilled its natural purpose – its 'final cause' or 'end'. When it comes to assessing tools, that approach is straightforward and works well: the box tells you what the tool is meant to do and you judge it according to whether it does it effectively. But how do you judge a human life? There is no purpose written on life's box; we have the daunting task of working out for ourselves whether we have a purpose and, if so, how we might fulfil it.

That, of course, assumes that the universe is in some way the product of rational design, whether religious or secular. If there is no pre-ordained design, then success is more a matter of survival than of function. Those best adapted to their environment survive and reproduce. Is that, then, the ultimate evolutionary criterion of success? To outbreed all others? To ensure that our genes are as widely disseminated as possible? History is littered with males who have taken just such a view.

So, if there is no designed criterion of success, we are thrown back onto the Nietzchian option of determining rather than discovering success. We say that the *Übermensch* shall be the meaning of the earth. All will follow from that decision. Success then becomes a matter of a battle of wills; we strive for what we want to achieve, recognizing that all others have the right to do the same. But Devil takes the hindmost. After all, in any capitalist system, all businesses strive to succeed, but can do so only because others are able to fail. In a competitive environment, success is in limited supply.

But there is another hazard waiting for those who crave success. It is the fate of the ambitious to slip straight from wannabe to has-been, discounting achievements in favour of plans. If your success is always to be achieved in the future, you will never quite achieve it, for as soon as you arrive at one goal, another will present itself. Only when, through old age, exhaustion or the more dynamic efforts of the next generation, you finally give up your ambition to be more, will you be in a position to appreciate what you have done. But, by then, you will already find that you are being sidelined and patronized by the up-and-coming who, driven by their own ambition, are determined to improve on your achievements and thereby discount them in your own eyes. The ambitious are always stalked, by their own fear of failure, if not by rivals.

The problem, of course, is that success is *retrospective* (a measure of where you have come from) while ambition is *prospective* (a measure of where you want to go). Both threaten an accurate assessment of the present, for the first makes it seem inevitable, failing to recognize how much of our success may be down to luck or circumstances, while the latter discounts the present in favour of the future, sacrificing what is now for what will become later. In many ways, the image of the successful and ambitious person is like that of the gambler. Having won a considerable sum, the temptation is to press on in hope of winning more. Leaving the gaming table when reasonably ahead might be a sensible option in terms of one's overall level of happiness, but success tends only to feed ambition and the onward march towards the promise of greater things.

However, if we are tempted to think that the ambitious, multi-tasking executive is a recent phenomenon, consider this passage in Nietzsche's *The Gay Science* (para. 329) written in 1887:

> 'One thinks with a watch in one's hand, even as one eats one's midday meal while reading the latest news of the stock market; one lives as if one always 'might miss out on something'.

'Virtue has come to consist in doing something in less time than someone else.'

'More and more, work enlists all good conscience on its side; the desire for joy already calls itself a "need to recuperate" and is beginning to be ashamed of itself. "One owes it to one's health" – that is what people say when they are caught on an excursion into the country.'

Originally, he argues, the noble tried to conceal the fact that they might need to work; work was contemptible, something for slaves. Now we regard it as a mark of success. Nietzsche would have had something to say about those who take their laptop on holiday (see Chapter 2).

When it comes to directing ambition, whether it be of an individual or a company, there is a temptation to rely on empirical facts. A Board, faced with tough decisions about the future direction of a company, needs to amass facts. If in doubt, it asks for more, sending the executives scuttling back to their spreadsheets. If the new detail does not resolve things, they may (often at great expense) go for the terminal option and bring in a statistician. At that point their cause is hopelessly lost. Why? Because the Board members have been working on the assumption that success and ambition are both directly related to data. Our profits are up! Does that automatically mean that we are successful? We want to grow and dominate the market! Is that either a realistic or desirable outcome of our efforts? The answer to both of these may be 'Yes', but that will depend on all sorts of issues about what the company is for and how it sees the value of what it does and for whom – issues that do not depend upon facts. If data could establish values, principles and direction, no company would need Directors, it could quite easily be operated by a computer.

It is commonplace to say that success (whether individual or corporate) is not related to wealth, or that one's ambition need not translate into measurable benefits. But beneath that corny affirmation is the fundamental division between fact and value. No amount of information about the past or projections concerning the future will, in themselves, determine what is the right policy for a company.

The statistician will never be able to illuminate the values by which your company operates, merely its success or otherwise within a market economy, or its ability to deliver on goals that have already been chosen.

And, of course, we always need to keep in mind the Sorites paradox (see Chapter 1). Between success and failure there are a million gradations and mediocrity comes in a wonderful range of shades. You'll need to be careful how you define success if you want to be convincing when you claim to have achieved it!

But without ambition nothing gets done; to see a possibility and work to make it a reality is the mark of a life directed by reason, so we should not mock the overtly ambitious. Equally, it would be arrogant not to acknowledge the comfort and reassurance that even the most modest success can bring. Both success and ambition have their place; but their qualities and promised satisfactions are addictive and potentially self-destructive. Their boxes should be labelled with the advice given by some manufacturers of alcoholic beverages: please enjoy responsibly.

AT HOME

As a personal exercise, plot out a mind map of your ambitions and your successes. Add in your failed ambitions for good measure. What were your ambitions at earlier stages of your life? Did things work out as you expected? Which matter most to you now? What do you consider realistic? Does realism matter?

If, as a result of this exercise, you determine to take more responsibility for shaping your own life, rather than accepting the norms of others, you might consider reading more on Existentialism, e.g. *Understand Existentialism*, by Nigel Rodgers and Mel Thompson (Hodder, Teach Yourself, 2010).

17

Did you bring your camera?

The joy of the small-format digital camera is that it enables you to capture the moment with ease, edit out the unwanted details in Photoshop, shrink the image to an appropriate size for emailing and then send it to your friends. Even the most fleeting experience can be captured and shared, if not with a camera, at least with a phone. How things have changed since aristocrats, arriving in Venice as part of their grand European tour, would commission a painting to commemorate their visit. Canaletto thrived on wealthy patrons who wanted to capture the moment.

But Canaletto also anticipated (in his own most wonderful style) the curse of the small digital camera, in that both he and it tend to make everything in the scene so sharp. That, of course, is no doubt what he, and those who market cameras today, parade as a virtue; people want sharp pictures. But tear your eyes away from the Canalettos as they hang in the gallery and observe for a moment those who are viewing them. They first stand back, taking in the scene, but almost immediately move forward to scan the painting, enjoying the small tableaux that are to be found in every corner, each detail revealing something of the life of the city. Some, like moles, almost sniff their way across the canvas, luxuriating in fine brushstrokes and acute observation. Take a Canaletto home from your travels and you have not one picture but a whole album. So also the small format camera, with its short focal length lens, can render everything sharp across the frame. The foreground characters are set against an equally sharp background that constantly distracts the eye. You are tempted, as with a Canaletto, to explore detail.

By contrast, the enthusiastic photographer will likely use a larger format and fixed focal length lens with a large aperture, hoping thereby to render the main subject sharp but set it against a softly blurred background. The idea is to enable the photograph to 'say something' to the extent that it leads the eye to what is important, detaching it from the background clutter of life, isolating and presenting it for inspection. Photography can be a creative way of seeing and presenting.

Hence the discussions today about the extent to which photography can be considered art on the same level as painting. Some would argue that it cannot, since the process of generating a photograph is essentially mechanical. Others see photography as the same as any other visual art, with the camera as an alternative to the pencil or brush, a tool through which the artistic perception can be expressed.

But the different styles of photography provide an insight into our habitual way of observing the world. The human eye is always selective, it scans the view, giving more attention to what is of interest, or danger, or attractiveness. It varies its exposure as it does so, opening up the iris to see what lurks in the shadows and shielding itself from the glare of the summer sky. The still photograph, even with enhancement technology, tends to average out both interest and exposure – you have to work hard, selecting the focal length of lens that will give the right perspective and aperture for deciding the depth of field, to enable your subject either to 'pop out of' or become lost within its background. The keen photographer is required to ask 'What needs to be sharp, what can best be hinted at in softer focus?' or 'Do I need to preserve the texture in the highlights here, or am I more interested in the shadow areas?'

Hence the value of taking a camera when travelling. It encourages a critical reflection on what is seen: What stands out here? What is explained by its context? What is it about the quality of light that makes this moment so special? How can it be captured? These questions become the basis for a philosophy of looking. What you see and what you wish to capture are a measure of your engagement with the scene.

The uncritical desire to capture information can be taken to extremes. Some years ago, we were about to leave the Beatles' exhibition in Liverpool, just as the museum was closing, when a crowd of tourists surged in and were disappointed to find that they could not be admitted beyond the gift shop. One young man, clamping a video camera to his eye, guided himself around the shop entirely through his viewfinder, looking up and down, left and right, the camera swaying with him. What will be the result? Apart from a mild nausea as the fixed screen captures the swaying and surging of his lens, it will also reflect exactly what he saw. All the rest of the experience, the sort of thing we pick up through peripheral vision, sounds, smells and so on, will have been eliminated. His single electronic eye will have narrowed his experience. He did not see the museum or even the museum shop – he only saw his digital viewfinder and its moving images. Like the prisoners in Plato's cave, he saw no more than shadows, far removed from reality.

The camera does not simply record the scene, it also records – for you as you look at the finished photo – your reason for taking the image. Framed groups of smiling faces are tokens of remembered friendship, relaxation and happiness. Each photograph, whether technically proficient or the simplest of amateur snaps, can 'say' something. If it does not, press the delete button!

We also remember through images. The family on holiday – cause of celebration or regret? Yes, that was the last holiday we had with her before she died (the image taking on a significance that could not have been known when the shutter was released). That was just before we had the children. That was when we celebrated retirement. Did I really wear those flares? Oh, no! Just look at my hair! And there is a surge of emotion, as the experience is recalled. For good or ill, a photograph revivifies experience and relationships. You see the image of someone long neglected and remember that you should call them. We are what we capture by way of images – our memory, jogged by photographs, keeps our dreams and fears alive, reminds us of what shaped our lives at the time the shutter was released.

But the image cannot fully reproduce what is before the camera. Take movement. We assume that, with a fast shutter speed, movement is 'frozen'. But in fact the blurring of the moving subject remains, it's just becomes too small for us to see. What you have in a single image is an approximation; in a movie you have a series of approximations, strung together to give the impression of continuous movement. But this is also the way in which we perceive things with the naked eye. After all, the stars in the sky appear to be fixed, but we know that the galaxies are moving away from one another at a fantastic speed, and that our own solar system is swinging on the arm of a galaxy. But our observation – through our lifetime, through all human lifetimes – is just too short for us to see the blur as the stars hurtle through the void. If photography is always an approximate summary of an experience, then experience itself is always an approximate summary of reality.

Why is photography so popular as a hobby? Perhaps because, with the speed at which we absorb new experiences, we need some way of holding onto those that are most important for us. Capture the moment? No that's impossible, the fact that moments pass and vanish forever is just a fact of life. Photography is the attempt to hold back that process; to retain enough of our past experience to remind us of the journey thus far and to affirm who we are. And I guess that, faced in lonely old age with the prospect of a bed in a nursing home with very limited space, my photographs would be my most precious possessions. So photographs of this beach moment may serve to remind you of this specific point in your life – it may indeed be the first or last of something; only time will tell.

Thoughtful photography sharpens perception; forcing you to consider what is significant and what is not, what is subject and what background – not unlike the act of evaluating your own life as you sit on your beach, trying to identify and isolate the significant from the endless stream of inessential clutter that forms the background to our life's image.

Photographs is just another way of doing philosophy. So did you bring your camera?

Can you shape your own context?

You can only understand a word because it has a context – a place within a language; on its own it is merely a sound, signifying nothing. The larger the dictionary in which you look up that word, the broader the context it describes and thus the more subtle the definition. But we appear to have a problem here:

- The definition can only be written because the word already has a meaning.
- But how can it have meaning without a definition?
- We listen to how a word is used, but since we can never hear all the occasions on which it is used, our understanding of that word must always remain provisional.
- So a definition is always going to be limited by the number of contexts it takes into account.

And this illustrates a more general point. You can best understand a part by looking at its place within the whole of which it is a part; but it may be equally true that you can best understand a whole in terms of the parts of which it is a whole. Between parts and wholes it's chicken and egg. This is sometimes referred to as the hermeneutic circle – hermeneutics being the study of how things are interpreted.

If, as you sit on your beach, you choose to reflect on who you are and what your life is about, you will sooner or later hit the problem of this hermeneutic circle. Were you to be on a psychiatrist's couch, or buried in a self-help manual, you yourself would be the focus of the enquiry. What is the real you? How can all those things in which you engage become expressions of who you are and what you want to become? How do you set your individual stamp on the place where you live, the circles of people among whom you move, or the work you do?

To be creative and interesting you need to make a *difference* to your environment, but equally, all that you are can be seen as the *product* of that environment. This is the stuff of every biography; to understand someone I need to appreciate their background, the influences on them in their formative years, the opportunities they were given and the resulting actions that displayed their developing character.

And so, if we try to analyse ourselves, we go round in circles: we contribute to the context of which we appear to be the product. In the biological world, growth and complexity can only develop within open systems – in other words, those that take energy in from outside themselves. You are an open system, constantly dependent upon oxygen, food, water, ideas, social acknowledgement, the acclaim of your peers.

Hence the folly of assuming that neuroscience can explain character. Character is not an entity to be analysed but an on-going process of interaction between self and context. As everyone who has ever been involved with gardening knows, plants can flourish only in the right environment. Hence those therapies and career advice sessions that seek to find the context to unlock happiness or potential. But equally, as anyone who has observed a growing child knows, progress comes by way of learning how to manipulate your environment. You are the product of that which you attempt (blatantly if you're a two year old; with varying degrees of subtlety if you're adult) to manipulate. We are so easily caught in a circle of interpretation: my free choice (even in the act of a simple retail purchase) will soon become a statistic which will in turn be used to explain my free choice.

Buddhist philosophy speaks of karma in terms of the natural results of thoughts and actions. Our thoughts of yesterday shape who we are today, and our present thoughts go to shape who we will be tomorrow. We are the product of our mind; each thought becomes the context within which the next thought makes sense. But that does not imply a rigid sequence of cause and effect. Rather, it suggests that our context is like water through which we swim, ever changing as we disturb it and move forward.

In many ways, this returns us to the old question about whether we *discover* our meaning through the things that surround us, or *create* it by constructing a story to say who we are. Much recent thought, especially that mixture of ideas that is labelled 'postmodernist', is highly suspicious of any metanarrative, any story that seeks to make sense of everything, fearing that it will distort that which it seeks to fit into too neat a conceptual scheme.

Do you generate existential angst for yourself by craving an overarching meaning for your life, or do you settle for contented superficiality? I would suggest that this is a bogus question. We do not have to choose between those options. In reality, we engage with and respond to our context; we thereby give ourselves character. We do not wait to have a defined character before we can engage with our context.

With hindsight, we see the context that has shaped us; looking forward, we have a measure of freedom to shape our own context.

AT HOME

Look up the distinctively Buddhist view of karma, or try a general introduction to Eastern Philosophy, such as my book *Understand Eastern Philosophy*, Teach Yourself Books, 2012.

19

Is fairness possible?

The first ethical comment to issue from the lips of most children is 'It's not fair!', coming some time after the first metaphysical question 'Why?' But in case you did not receive a satisfactory response to your complaint, or have long since forgotten what that complaint was, let us briefly consider whether fairness is ever possible.

So where do you start?

- *Liberals* (including economic liberals) tend to start with the autonomy of the individual – everybody is allowed to do their own thing, as long as doing it does not impede the right of everyone else to do the same. In this context 'It's not fair!' implies that my right to do what I want, based perhaps on seeing others able to do it when I can't, means that my autonomy of action has been frustrated.
- *Utilitarians* take the democratic approach and allow the majority to decide what is fair – thus allowing minorities to be treated unfairly. And if unfairness persists, particularly in countries that are undemocratic, then the greatest good for the greatest number may need to be imposed by force.

* *Communitarians*, by contrast, consider that who we are as individuals is defined to a significant extent by the society within which we live. Society makes us who we are, but birth often determines where we shall be in the social and economic pecking order. At its extreme, it might suggest that if I claim that society is unfair, I haven't understood what is in my own best interest.
* *Egalitarians* insist that it is only fair for all to be treated alike, even if what is fair is liked by some and not by others. Whole economies have been planned on that basis, and few have been happy with the result.
* *Marxists* claim that the only fair way to operate is for each to give according to ability and take according to need, which sounds fine but never quite rang true of Marxist societies.

OK, so each of these is a caricature, the serious nuancing of which would take far longer than most people will remain on their beach – but let them simply highlight the range of options open to anyone trying to sort out the question of fairness or justice in society.

But what we see as fair also reflects the story we want to tell about society as a whole and what it stands for. Michael Sandal, for example, has a 'narrative communitarian' approach. He thinks that we all have our own moral values and ideas, and that we bring these to our social awareness. We have a 'collective narrative' about who we are and what we want as a society. This makes the question of fairness one that requires something of a dialogue between individuals and society. If I think certain things are right or fair or just, that reflects my appreciation of what society is about, and my expression of those things contributes to the ongoing debate, which in turn shapes society. Fairness is an iterative process.

Justice, of course, has been a central question in philosophy since Plato tackled it in *The Republic*, but in the 1970s the debate was kick-started by John Rawls, whose book *A Theory of Justice* argued for 'justice as fairness', taking a liberal egalitarian view and critical of the utilitarian approach. At the heart of his argument is a thought experiment.

Rawls considers what the result would be if you gathered together a group of people to decide on a fair distribution of resources, but placed them behind a 'veil of ignorance' so that they did not know anything about themselves. They can say what is in their best interests, but they do not know if they are old or young, rich or poor, male or female. They have no idea about their needs nor about what they have to contribute. They are in what Rawls calls the 'original position'. In this situation, what will they opt for?

He believes that, looking at the logic of the situation, they will opt for two things:

* That each person should have equal rights to the most extensive system of liberty, provided that it does not prevent others from having similar liberties.
* That, if there are to be any inequalities in the distribution of resources, such inequalities should always be such as to benefit the least advantaged in society, and also that all should have a fair and equal opportunity to secure offices and positions.

In other words, to put it crudely, you'd play it safe! If you find yourself on the top of the heap, you have less to lose than those at the bottom have to gain. But you might be on the bottom, in which case, on balance, it's going to be safest to bias towards the poor.

There are many criticisms of Rawls, which are beyond our present reflection, but one is crucial. What he has here is a thought experiment, and one that depends on an impossibility. In reality, people know where they stand in the pecking order and their views cannot help but take that into account. Taking an objective view of things, when it comes to questions of fairness, is practically impossible. Even the most determined egalitarian is likely to say that everyone should be able to have just a little more than he or she (the speaker) has at the moment. Few would want to take the sort of radical steps advocated by radical ethical thinkers such as Peter Singer, and deliberately take a drastic cut in living standards to benefit the poorest, or indeed the planet as a whole.

The other problem with Rawls' approach is that people like to gamble, and many would rather take a chance on doing really well than play it safe. In free market economics, nobody opts for the weakest companies to be protected from predators.

Several spanners can be thrown into the egalitarian works. Human nature dictates that people are incentivized by rewards; we work in order to improve the lot of ourselves and our families. And on that score, of course, it takes a degree of moral heroism to be equally concerned about our nearest and dearest and anonymous people who suffer in other parts of the world. Bonds of kinship run deep. In other words, an argument can be made for the idea that human nature has a selfish element to it, and that any radical redistribution of the world's resources would require an unrealistic shift in attitudes.

Unfairness at the extremes is easy to spot – whether it's a banker's bonus on the one hand or the death of a child for lack of a cheap vaccine on the other. What is far more difficult is to see how you could legislate for a fairer society without the risk of human nature always finding a way around what justice might suggest to be the fairest option.

Self-sacrifice has always been seen as a laudable quality in the Western saint, the Buddha-to-be, or the Zen sage, but few are able to put it into practice, and those who do are sometimes accused of neglecting their family, for example, in order to 'do good' elsewhere. More common is the view of Thomas Hobbes that society is there to prevent the life of unfettered competition from being 'nasty, brutish and short', or of Marx, that people are regarded as cogs in an economic wheel, alienated from what they produce in order to generate profits for the owners of capital.

A quest for fairness touches on so many other philosophical questions. Cultural relativism suggests that each society should be free to organize itself according to its own traditions. But what do we say if those traditions are, for example, unfair on women? Do we then go for an absolute view of fairness and set aside our cultural sensitivities?

Even among those of approximately equal economic rank there can be issues of fairness. Whether it's on a cruise ship or in a hotel, people may eye one another up and down wondering who paid full price for this trip and who secured the last-minute crazy discount price. One person's unfairness is another person's bargain.

And what of fairness on and around your beach? There are resorts where the holidaymaker is effectively isolated from the surrounding population. Can you afford this holiday only because minimal wages are being paid to those who work to make your stay pleasant? In a bijou resort in Thailand, I was delighted to find flower petals on the bed, but horrified to find that the lawns and shrubs were being manicured by an army of gardeners using clippers. Eyes down, they clipped away as we walked to the pool. Where's the justice in that? But there again, if there were no tourists, what work would there be for them? And what has it done to their society? And so on, and so on. As we ponder questions of fairness, we relate particular situations to an overall story we tell ourselves about what life should ideally be like, both for ourselves and for others.

And so we swing between socially imposed fairness options, and the freedom of individuals to set their own agendas. Does the answer lie in some 'big society' option where the better off contribute of their bounty and time for the benefit of others? Or is that to abdicate the responsibility of government to seek fairness for all? And to what extent is fair treatment dependent upon conformity or effort? Do all deserve to be treated alike? What of those who are themselves unfair – either by exploiting others for their own gain and protecting their high salaries at one end of the scale, or cheating on the benefit system at the other? Are we required to be fair in our treatment of the unfair?

Perhaps we don't know and can't know what's fair in any absolute sense; the best we can do is act on what seems so, trying in a limited way to get back behind Rawls' 'veil of ignorance' in order to remove the most egocentric of perspectives.

AT HOME

Read *Justice* by Michael Sandal (Allen Lane, 2009) or log on to his lectures on Justice at Harvard, available free on the web. You may not agree with him, but he presents the issues of justice and fairness with consummate clarity.

Or, for a general introduction to political philosophy, with a chapter on the quest for equality and fairness, see my *Understand Political Philosophy* (Teach Yourself, 2010).

20

Waiting for the ferry?

The harbour at Dover is hardly inspirational. Shunting in line as we wait for our ferry on the swathes of concrete that push out into the Channel from beyond the white cliffs, it is more often than not simply a matter of avoiding diesel fumes and killing time before loading.

But there is also surely a slight frisson, contemplating the journey ahead, clipping the beam adjusters onto the car headlights, sticking a GB badge on the back of the car, checking the map. This is a place of hope, of anticipation, of anxiety perhaps, and also of finality as one country is left behind and another anticipated. It is also, of course, the place illegal immigrants dream of as they try to stow away, a place of human traffic as well as freight and holidaymakers. For most people, Dover is not a place naturally associated with honeymoons, but for one Victorian poet it provided exactly the image he needed.

Looking out of one's hotel bedroom window on honeymoon, savouring the night air, is surely the archetypal moment for relaxed, post-coital contentment. Yet Matthew Arnold, looking out from his hotel bedroom in Dover, probably in the June of 1851, sees the lights out in the straights and hears the 'long withdrawing roar' of the waves on the shingle, and in that moment fashions one of the defining images of a generation aware of the loss of traditional certainties, his poem 'On Dover Beach'.

For him the sea was no longer a comforting mantle furled round the earth, but the symbol of a bleak, confrontational future in which armies clash at night (the most foolish of all military strategies, in days before night-vision glasses, fighting an enemy in the dark). He glimpsed at that moment, a cultural and philosophical shift in his generation, away from the comforts of faith, and sees that loss not as liberation but as heralding a colder and more uncertain future.

There is much to be explored in that poem, which gives such a wonderful glimpse into the heart of the 19th century. Ideas can latch onto images found in the most unlikely of times and places, so don't despise the transit lounge or ferry port, though hardly the most aesthetically pleasing of places, for they too may inspire. But what, in more prosaic form, shall we make of them now?

First of all, they are also great places for people watching, observing the strategies of those who are determined that their holiday will start right now, those who are inspired by last-minute shopping opportunities, families settling down to the challenging prospect of a couple of weeks in close proximity, and the occasional lost soul in dark suit and briefcase, tapping into his or her computer, and trying to ignore the general holiday-anticipating hubbub. And, if the sense of people coming and going to their various destinations is not sufficient for an image of life itself, there are always the police with their sub-machine guns, protecting us all from the moment when someone else's philosophy is imposed upon us with deadly intent.

Ships leaving port have long embodied in literature or song the sense of starting out on a journey, leaving behind the familiar – whether it's the leaving of Liverpool that grieves me, or the tap tap tap, as a blind man takes his final steps on land before boarding Ahab's ship and the desperate quest for Moby Dick. Casting off is a moment of existential commitment; the journey has begun.

But here, contemplating the Dover tarmac, we may also reflect on the shortness of a single human life in the greater scheme of geological time. Only 6,000 years ago (a mere blink in global terms) we could have walked from here over into France or across to the Netherlands and Northern Germany. Nothing is fixed, the traumas of separation that afflicted our Mesolithic ancestors as sea levels rose flooding the planes and then the islands that once occupied what is now the North Sea are long in the past, but perhaps we also recognize that even the lapping of water on Dover Beach, little changed since Matthew Arnold's time, will some day be no more. There are changes so profound and slow that we feel we can safely ignore them as we queue for the ferry.

AT HOME

Read Matthew Arnold's 'On Dover Beach'.

21

Was there once upon a time?

Time is a feature of the way we experience things. It may be measured in terms of the regular passing of hours and days, but it is not experienced like that; rather, everything is tensed – belonging to our past (if we remember it), present (if we can catch its fleeting passage) or the future we anticipate.

Nor is time experienced as uniform. In excitement, it passes in a flash; in drudgery it drags out into a boredom in which time itself seems to stop. The child waking up to realize that it is his or her birthday, does not think that this is just any day. The Jew, celebrating the Seder Supper, asks 'Why is this night different from all other nights?' and begins to unfold the narrative of the escape from Egypt. A birth, marriage or death warp the significance of an otherwise uniform span of time. A day may be etched forever in the memory, while years may pass of which, thinking back, we remember little.

Our life is like a narrative with key points that shape our story. We live, as we read, not knowing what will happen next, always anticipating. The story makes sense only as we stop and recollect its twists and turns.

But time is not just experienced in the significant events but also in the routine patterns of change. We feel its imprint in the turning of the seasons, the approach of anniversaries, the anticipation of familiar events. The end of September always reminds me of undergraduate days and the buzz of leaving the quiet of my country home for the stimulus of city and university life. For me, therefore, the first chill of autumn brings more anticipation than regret. Camping in the south of France one September, our tent covered with prematurely browned and fallen leaves at the end of a hot, dry summer, I suddenly wanted to be heading home. Now, on reflection, I realize it was nothing to do with a waning of holiday pleasures, but the half-conscious memory of falling leaves and the anticipated excitement of the academic life. The first flakes of snow or the opening of spring buds are natural phenomena, but they are more – they are glimpses into the slipping of one season into memory and anticipation of the next.

The simplest of actions can trigger a story of the passing of time. Picking blackberries along a hedgerow suddenly reminds me of doing so with my grandmother as a child, and brings a longing for all that has gone and regret at the passing of all those years in which I have been too preoccupied with other things to notice that it had become blackberry time again.

We do not simply 'have' a past and a future, we 'are' the past and the future – our history and our hopes define who we are now. Applying for a job, we are required to display the CV of our past, and to share our hopes for the future, to see if they are in line with the hopes of the prospective employer. Don't try telling the employment agency that your past no longer exists and is therefore irrelevant. The past is an essential part of the present. Nor should you suggest that you are unconcerned about the non-existent future, for they will regard you as lacking motivation and hopeless.

The experience of time invites autobiography. We look back at events and weave them into a pattern in order to make sense of our lives. The past is not just a sequence of events, but is a narrative that starts with our own personal 'once upon a time' and attempts to make sense out of who we are now.

Hence, I think, the fascination with stories. Religions record and rehearse stories to show how the universe and human life has come to be as it is, and those who are not hung up on literalist interpretations recognize that creation stories are a way of expressing values and making sense, rather than giving information about ancient pre-history. The stories told by playwrights and novelists give shape to random events, show influences, develop and flesh out characters, give depth to historical periods. As we become engrossed when reading a well-crafted or fast-paced novel, we become part of the story, we identify with it and learn from it.

Is any of this significant for philosophy? Absolutely! When we talk about value, or morality, or happiness or meaning and purpose – or all the other human considerations that spring from them, like justice, aesthetic appreciation, religion – we are not dealing with entities that can be appreciated exclusively in terms of data that can be measured in the present. To understand another person, we cannot rely on brain scans or x-rays; we need a story, a narrative that includes experiences and responses and the values and habitual ways of seeing and thinking that spring from them. To say who we are, we need to start with 'Once upon a time'. To reflect on who we have become, we perhaps need to look back and find that point from which our present story has evolved.

We don't need analysis to show the importance of childhood experience, nor is it hard to see the way in which trauma can shape subsequent life. Nor do we need to read Proust to appreciate that we carry with us the conscious and unconscious residue of experience. It is that residue, ever changing with subsequent living, which is the process by which the passage of time shapes who we are. The personal, existential questions on which we have been reflecting in this book are all set in the context of our story.

So perhaps the time you spend on your beach is as good as any other for reflecting on the story that explains your present self, and of those significant moments when you have 'seen' what life is about, moments that explain how things turned out as they did.

Shall we get to know one another as we sit on our beach together? There is only one way in which we can effectively set about doing so. Are you sitting comfortably? Then it's time to begin: 'Once upon a time …'

Draw up a time line of your life so far, and mark on it the people, places and events that have been significant in shaping you. That simple exercise, valuable in itself for reminding you of your story, is also an illustration of the way in which time is not uniform but related to events of significance. Have you lost any years? Were there moments, the import of which remain with you to this day? And at what point does your present story start?

22

Is any theory as good as any other?

As opposed to politics or religion, where commitment is expected, it is the hallmark of good science that it remains intellectually flexible, always willing to revise its theories in the light of new evidence. But that flexibility does not generally extend to saying that any theory is as good as any other, even if there are occasions when two theories have an equal claim to explain the evidence. If a theory emerges as being more useful, more able to explain apparent anomalies in the evidence, simpler, more elegant, or wider in its application than the others, it displaces them.

But theories are not always easy to displace. In his hugely influential book *The Structure of Scientific Revolutions*, 1962, Thomas Kuhn challenged the view (held by Karl Popper and others) that a theory should always be open to falsification and should be discarded or modified once evidence emerges that contradicts its predictions. Instead, he introduced the idea of the 'paradigm' – the set of widely accepted theories within which scientists work for most of the time.

New theories generally fit in with existing ones and thus strengthen the paradigm, but now and then something remarkable happens and a theory emerges which challenges the whole paradigm. When that happens, the paradigm is gradually weakened and its constituent theories undermined, until it finally gives way and you may have a 'paradigm shift'. Let's look at two such shifts:

* When Copernicus and later Galileo presented the idea that the Earth revolved round the sun, the Earth was displaced from the central place it had within the old paradigm of the cosmos. Suddenly a new vista opened up, in which the Earth became just one planet among others, a small and not remarkable object within what we later came to see as a vast and expanding universe.
* Equally, when Einstein put forward his theories of relativity, the old world of Newtonian physics suddenly seemed very limited in its application, and a new paradigm emerged with much wider application.

The dilemma is that we always think within the framework of accepted ideas, values and principles that we inherit from the society around us. They form our paradigm. To see things differently takes effort.

In life, as in science, there are paradigm shifts. The Reformation and Enlightenment in Europe saw a huge shift away from the acceptance of authority and towards the autonomy of the individual and the recognition of the value of logical argument. That shift affected not just religion, but politics, science and industry. By the 18th century, people thought very differently from those of the 15th or 16th.

Some political ideas create their own paradigm, within which everything else is interpreted. The ideas of Karl Marx were hugely influential from the 19th century to the collapse of the Communist states at the end of the 20th. Half the world lived within that paradigm. Then the whole radical socialist and communist system of ideas started to crumble and fall away. It was a massive social and political experiment with its own key ideas and values, and providing its own justification. In the end – if, indeed, there is an end, ideas can always be revived – the communist view lost out to global capitalism and individualism. It lost out, that is, in terms of the power and economic clout it could muster, and the degree to which it satisfied the aspirations of its peoples. Given that there were alternative paradigms available, people were able to compare them and make a choice – and that is exactly what they did in Eastern Europe and elsewhere.

Now we find that the general capitalist paradigm (including its natural extension in terms of the freedom to trade in financial derivatives) is under pressure. It finds its own points of weakness – the banking crisis and global recession has revealed some of them – and tries to deal with them from within the framework of its own ideas. But those who live within the paradigm find it incredibly difficult to shake off its basic assumptions. It is only natural that, even after a traumatic period, banks and other institutions will start to revert to their old habits.

And here is the problem. Kuhn pointed out that there was no way to judge between paradigms. The values of paradigm A suggest that paradigm B is useless; those of B refute the claims of A – just as, at one time, the capitalist and communist worlds confronted one another. But if we all live within one or other paradigm, can we genuinely make a choice? Is there some way of getting beyond the grip of the paradigm? Clearly, on the political front, that certainly happened with the fall of communism. It was because people saw that things could be different that they claimed the right to shift paradigm.

So let's extend Kuhn's principle. We have already considered political paradigms, but what about religion? Does it help to think of religions as paradigms?

Within the Christian paradigm, whether literally true or not, there are a number of beliefs and values that hold together around some key ideas – God, life beyond death, the example of Jesus of Nazareth, the mutual support offered by a Christian community, the duty to help those in need and so on. Once living within that paradigm, your Christian ideas naturally colour all that you encounter. Your political allegiance, your work, your relationships – all will be seen from within that religious paradigm.

On the other hand, someone who opts for an atheist-humanist paradigm will naturally champion the value of rational argument, the autonomy of the individual, the moral responsibility conferred by virtue of being alive as a human being. That paradigm naturally rejects all it sees as superstition, just as the Christian paradigm tends to reject the atheist as lacking any ultimate sense of value or meaning in life. But it does no good for the religious person to argue that his or her beliefs have been misunderstood, thinking that this will sway the atheist critic, or vice versa. They have indeed been misunderstood, but simply because they have been evaluated from within a conflicting paradigm.

The snag with political and religious paradigms, as with scientific ones, is how to compare them objectively. Hence some may be tempted to give up any attempt to claim that there can ever be a right or wrong, or any absolute value, in political or religious views. This leads to the whole problem of multiculturalism. Each culture brings its own values and traditions, and it is impossible to get a genuinely neutral standpoint from which to assess them. Multiculturalism sometimes celebrated 'our common humanity' to which the rich variety of cultures contribute. But that idea of humanity is itself a paradigm; it is a structure by which we are able to see ourselves as a single human family. Is that paradigm essential for the future? Is it the paradigm of all paradigms in social, religious and political terms? Only time will tell.

Nevertheless there are those who say that certain things (basic human freedoms, for example) form that bedrock of ideas that lie beneath the differing cultures, and by which the latter may therefore be judged. Equally, people will argue that, beneath the humanist celebration of the value of human life and the religious person's idea of God, there is some fundamental sense of the value and transcendent quality of life. And for the scientific realist, there is the conviction that, for all the different theories and paradigms on offer, the quest is to understand reality a bit better through our efforts.

So is any theory as good as any other? They can only be evaluated in terms of the paradigm within which they are set. The bigger question is whether any paradigm is as good as any other? And once you ask that question, you launch yourself into a multi-faith, multi-cultural, multi-political debate that will run and run.

This will always be frustrating for the person who craves certainty. But the option is to claim to have achieved certainty, only to find that the paradigm within which you have done so begins to crumble. Even asking whether something is 'as good as' another is problematic – for 'good' is determined by the values of the paradigm. What is good for one person might well be bad for another; a good socialist and a good capitalist each bring to the discussion their respective paradigms.

So how do we get beyond this circle of frustration? The answer may lie in the way in which paradigms are replaced within science. It is clear, for example, that when Newtonian physics was challenged by Einstein's theories of relativity, it was not thereby shown to be false, only that its ability to predict accurately operated within a limited set of parameters. On the surface of the Earth for most objects of the size we deal with on a daily basis (leaving out what happens when particles are smashed together in the accelerator at CERN), Newton works perfectly well, thanks. Newtonian physics does not deal with big bangs, black holes or sub-atomic particles and its mechanical view of the world may now have been replaced by one described by quantum mechanics and relativity, but it remains fine for many practical purposes.

We may need to settle for the fact that some theories are useful even if they do not give the ultimate or comprehensive picture of reality, and that the best of our theories are likely to be modified or replaced at some point in the future. Meanwhile, we have to live with the fact that we cannot always decide whether any one theory is better than any other, without qualifying that judgement as coming from within our own personal, political, religious or scientific paradigm.

AT HOME

For a good introduction to the issue of theories and paradigms, see *Kuhn Vs. Popper: The Struggle for the Soul of Science* by Steve Fuller (Icon Books, 2003).

23

Do you believe your own website?

At one time, only stars or those wealthy or politically powerful enough to justify the attentions of a PR consultant would have their public image enhanced. Now, thanks to the internet, we can all have our corner of cyberspace and with it an opportunity to present ourselves to the world, whether on Facebook, a website or even by morphing ourselves into a avatar and striding out into a virtual environment. We can at last show ourselves as we think we are (or would like to be) rather than having to accept what other people perceive us to be.

And that's what makes the web so liberating. We decide who we are, and present ourselves to anyone interested in seeing a list of our interests, hopes, ambitions, where we went to school, where we work, our favourite films, book or whatever, along with the photos we choose to publish and links to friends and organizations. In short, by publishing on the web, we are able to create and promote the metanarrative of our life, the story that sums up who we are and what we wish to be, our self-chosen viewpoint from which others can admire us.

The website becomes a personal showcase, and you can surf the net to find out about other people. But do you believe what you read on their sites? Has their career really followed that smooth upward trajectory; are their marriages that perfect or their children that talented? From time to time, browsing other people's sites, there comes that mild nausea induced by reading other people's Christmas letters – a mixture of envy, disbelief and a sense of relative personal failure, mixed with a feeling of superiority for not having sent out such a letter oneself. Do you believe their websites? Should they believe your own?

You may try to be rational and honest – to present yourself as you hope others see you anyway. But are you the best judge of that? There is a huge gap between what others see of us and what we believe ourselves to be. I may sense that I know myself better than anyone else, simply because I know my own thoughts and intentions – things that others have to deduce from my speech, action and writing, or read in my expressions and body language. But is that a real assessment of who I am, or a fantasy that I hope to maintain? Which are more real – my thoughts or my actions, my intentions or my achievements? I may claim to be honest, but is that more a matter of wanting to be honest? I want to be the person I present to you on my site.

But beneath those questions and issues lie more fundamental ones: Is it ever possible to sum up and present our own life? Why would we want to do so? The web gives us the ability to shape and present ourselves as we wish to be, rather than as we are. But is that image any less honest because it is shaped by our ambitions for ourselves? Our intentions – both real and virtual – express our hopes, values and ideals. But surely these are the very things that define us as individuals. We are not just what we have become, but also what we hope for, for the self spans both past, present and future. So we 'are' the person on the website – this is who we wish to be, who we feel ourselves to be. Is that not also a relevant presentation? I may be more interested in where you are going than in where you have been.

It's hardly surprising that *Desert Island Discs* has been such a long-running radio show; autobiography has a special appeal, particularly when – by linking music into a biographical sequence – you get a comforting structure into which to slip the more personal aspects of the castaway's life. Like the traditional whodunit, biography offers life as a rounded, meaningful whole. Autobiography is always a bit more suspect – particularly if it is written by a politician – simply because few can resist the temptation to justify themselves and settle a few old scores in the process. Autobiography is more PR in its intention, telling a story that is deliberately tailored to create the required effect. But it seems to me that we need to tell stories about ourselves, to fend off existential angst; let me explain …

Although perhaps something of a caricature, it remains true that for most people in medieval society, personal identity and self-awareness were pretty much fixed. You were born to work a patch of land, and that – give or take the changes and chances of war, pestilence, and the whim of your lord – was where you stayed. You trained into a craft and stayed working at it throughout you life. Or you were born into a more elevated social position, as an elder son taking over the estate or a younger son heading for a career in the Church. You were a daughter waiting for the suitable marriage, or a widow scraping out an existence, hoping for charity. Your essence and social position were clear.

Then we have the changes of the Renaissance, the Reformation and the Enlightenment, when the intellectual goalposts of the medieval world changed and the writing and thinking classes shifted towards a greater appreciation of the role of the individual. Ordinary working people took to religious and political debating, enthusiasts 'ranted' round the countryside. And from that time there has been an increasing sense that the individual matters, and that each person should be free to present and represent themselves and their ideas as they see best, encouraged by democracy and the emancipation of slaves and women. By the mid 20th century, the traumas of war threw up an interest in existentialism – the idea that one did not have a fixed essence, but shaped one's life by one's own decisions and took responsibility for it. But the challenge of becoming a self-defining, authentic individual was never an easy option. It is far easier to have an essence and try to live up to it, than to be a blank sheet upon which one's decisions and personal choices attempt to sketch some sort of image. To affirm yourself without retreating behind a mask, a role or a fixed essence demands courage, as the existentialists were quick to point out. It produces angst; if I can be anything, I can also be nothing. Too much freedom makes you dizzy. But the existentialists insisted that you had no option but to take responsibility for shaping yourself through the process of living. Your life is what you make of it, just that.

But if existentialism claims that existence precedes essence, the web appears to offer the reverse. There I can present my essence, the image of who I believe myself to be. My task, if I am honest, is to try to live up to it. But at least the personal website offers a way out of existential angst; we look at it and remember our essence. The web gives us the possibility of presenting ourselves along with our skills, employments and social circles. It is, in effect, a way of staking out a place for ourselves within cyberspace.

But, whether believable or not, the website might actually have a positive role in developing who we are. The Buddha argued that our thoughts of today shape who we will be tomorrow. If our website image is an expression of what we aspire to be, rather more than what we have already become, then it may actually serve as a catalyst for our own self-development. Indeed, one technique in Mahayana Buddhist mediation is to visualize yourself as already being an enlightened being; imagining that you regard the world through enlightened eyes is a way of moving towards enlightenment. If so – to use a rather cynical example – it's a process not unlike that by which politicians gradually get to look more and more like their cartoons!

So do you believe your own website? Or do you believe that your website is what you wish to be?

AT HOME

Consider how you present yourself on the web, or through social media sites. Is your image there a summary or an aspiration?

24

Naked thoughts?

George Formby got his cheeky implications wrong. In his _Hi-Tiddly-Hi-Ti Island_ (a Pacific beach paradise with fantasy images to rival Gaugin, but without the latter's sinister side) he offers what appears to be an escalating scale of sexual provocation when he suggests that 'the girls there are all full of sport' leading to 'and wear their frocks a trifle short', and ending with 'and some are simply wrapped in thought' in Hi-Tiddly-Hi-Ti Isle. Trouble is, it doesn't quite work like that – and never did, not even in the 1950s when he recorded the song. No; when it comes to nakedness, glimpses of flesh and wisps of material are always going to be more sexy than straightforward, in-your-face, all-shapes-and-sizes-accepted nakedness.

We've already looked at paradise, so what about nakedness? Should the genuine philosopher, straining to appreciate the existential implications of being alive, prefer to be naked on the beach?

Among 'textiles', nakedness is associated with sex; but among the naturist fraternity it is just the most beautiful and natural way to be. Feeling the breeze and sun on your body, outside with no clothes on, you feel 'in' the world in a way that the clothed cannot. Even under an overcast sky, with a breeze whipping in off the water, there is something wonderful and liberating about displaying your goose bumps to the universe at large.

And clothes are problematic anyway. They make social and existential statements that may or may not reflect the reality of who we are. Uniforms take away our individuality and encourage us to conform to the social role they represent. A major feature of the ingenuity of British teenagers lies in modifying their school uniform in a way that is provocative and rebellious while remaining just about within the letter of the school law. But clothes make statements in so many ways: the hijab and burqa, the veil, the clerical collar, the punk outfit, the studded leather jacket, the judge's wig. Clothes are eloquent. But are they necessarily honest? Martin Heidegger, in his *Being and Time* (caution: this is a great book, but not an easy read), argued that we are often tempted to adopt particular social masks rather than being ourselves, to play a role rather than act with authenticity. Clothes play a large part in affirming such masks.

Clothes may also reflect the wearer's attitude. The extreme example of this is the dandy (the title also of a new book from Nigel Rodgers). He makes the point that dandyism is not simply a matter of fastidiousness of dress, it is a way of thinking about oneself, an aloofness of thought and behaviour, an elevated state of mind. At a more mundane level, designer labels perform the same function – they say more about you than flesh ever can.

But there is a negative side to nakedness, for it is associated with death and with poverty. We are encouraged in the New Testament to clothe the naked as a means of giving them basic aid, and none can forget the terrible images of naked bodies piled up in heaps at Auschwitz. To choose to be naked is one thing, to have it imposed is quite another. Those who are naked have no status, they reveal their human vulnerability; to humiliate someone, first remove their clothes.

But ever since Adam and Eve were said to feel shame at their nakedness, and reached for the fig leaves, a minority of religious people have been trying to regain their lost innocence. A major dispute within the Jain community in its early days was whether monks should remain naked ('sky clad' was the delightful term used) or accept a simple form of clothing. Some became clothed, but nakedness remained the ideal. Nakedness for the Jain is a sign of renunciation, of absolute simplicity and innocence. Those who have nothing, not even clothes, symbolize the value of non-possessiveness. And that, of course, holds true for the long tradition of naked asceticism within Indian religions. Of course, the temperature helps; naked ascetics do not thrive in polar regions.

Simplicity is one thing, innocence another, and the quest for innocence through nakedness is best exemplified in the Adamites, a 17th-century English sect who undressed to worship. Nakedness expressed innocence, absolute equality (and, no, we're not talking physical features of a personal kind) and open honesty within the community. They saw it as a return to the Garden of Eden, a celebration of what humankind was meant to be, going naked and unashamed before God.

So, as you look about you on your literal or metaphorical beach, consider what the textiles are saying with their clothes, however casual or minimal; from designer gear to distressed jeans, clothes are eloquent at presenting a personal image that may or may not be the truth about the wearer. Clothes categorize people and therefore also divide them. By contrast, there is a natural camaraderie on a naturist beach.

And if philosophy, particularly of the existentialist sort, includes exploring who we are and how we relate to the world and to other people, affirming ourselves in honesty and acting with authenticity, would it not be better if philosophers remained naked? Weather permitting!

AT HOME

Getting naked and wandering around the house may be a first step, but for the real sense of what naturism is about you need to be outdoors and, ideally, in the company of other people. Just try it! Walking naked down a beach and into the sea is a most liberating experience!

Or, to appreciate that clothes are about more than just looking good, read *The Dandy* by Nigel Rodgers.

25

Is there a world 'out there'?

There was a popular song, known only to older readers, whose lyrics I dare not reproduce for copyright reasons, but which went something along the lines of there being nothing I can do or say, but wiggle my toes in the sand and dream, because – and this is the significant bit – the world is a thousand miles away. That's wonderful as a song about the detached feeling of the beach, but it's hardly good philosophy. First of all, the world is too much with us – and no, not the world of the getting and spending in which we run the risk of laying waste our powers – but for the simple reason that we cannot escape it. We may be a thousand miles from our usual locus, but it is the same world that we see. Or is it? And is it the same 'me' that looks out on that world?

Wittgenstein, that master of brevity, declared that 'The subject self does not belong to the world: rather, it is the limit of the world' (*Tractatus*, 5:632). There is nothing in your visual field that corresponds to the eye with which you see. And that, as we have already observed, raises all the issues about the self in relation to the world and the nature of consciousness. Yet it also introduces another, very different way of looking at the world. Wittgenstein takes the spectator position: the world is 'out there'.

That raises questions. If all we know of the world is by way of our sense experiences, and if those experiences are reducible to sets of neurons firing in my brain, how do I know that there is a world 'out there' in reality. After all, I could at this moment be dreaming. Bishop Berkeley (1685–1753) argued that, since we cannot know that things continue to exist unless we perceive them, the world needed a constantly perceiving God in order to establish its on-going existence. Yet Samuel Johnson, asked by Boswell about Berkeley's view that the universe cannot be proved to exist except in our perceptions, dismissed the question in robust fashion by kicking a stone, saying 'I refute him thus!' Surely there is nothing more certain than that there is a world out there. And it's generally true that, when an answer seems to be nonsense, the question is generally wrong. So what's so wrong in asking if there's a world 'out there'?

Actually, Samuel Johnson's response is more philosophically sound than one might imagine. The key to discovering existence is to engage with it. What he is saying, albeit mainly with his foot, is that the world is what we engage with. I make a difference by kicking the stone, and that difference to things is what we mean when we say that the world exists. It is something with which we can get to grips. If it existed only in our minds, there would be nothing with which to interact.

Consciousness suggests that there is a world 'out there', but only because it reflects upon itself and assumes that there is another world 'in here'. In fact, of course, there is only one world, of which we are a part. All entities within that world are known by their boundaries – that is the way we distinguish one thing from another, it enables them to 'stand out' or 'exist'. We also have our boundaries (of which you will be especially aware if, exploring the implications of the last question in this book, you are sitting naked upon your beach, feeling the breeze on your flesh) beyond which our senses probe. But a physical analysis of things no more stops at our boundary than at any other. We are a bit of organized matter, no different in kind from that which is found throughout the universe – the atoms of which we are made long pre-dated us and will long survive us; we are but their temporary arrangement. When Johnson kicked the stone, he unwittingly avoided the dualist trap of separating off 'inner' and 'outer' reality and thereby seeing the latter as problematic. We know we are part of the world because we react to and influence other parts of the world – we kick the stone and feel the pain in our foot. That's reality – the inter-connectedness of things. The question should not be 'does the world exist' but 'Why should I assume that I exist separate from the rest of the world?'

Martin Heidegger, a 20th-century almost-unreadable philosophical giant, explores the same issue in *Being and Time*, but his answer is predictably less succinct than Johnson's! He points to the fact that we are 'thrown' into life at a particular time and place; we are embedded, and deal with things that come to our hand in a practical and engaged way. To be human is to have a world; our experience of the world is always also an experience of ourselves within it. (That doesn't start to do justice to Heidegger's argument – if you want more, just take up the challenge of engaging with his work.)

The problem is, however much we are able to show a physical continuum between the objects we perceive, our senses and our brain, we always actually experience in 'dualist' mode; we look out on the world. Our senses mediate a relationship between our 'self' and that which we perceive. But experience is a double-facing phenomenon: we *experience* something, and we experience *something*; neither works without the other. Experience cannot be contained within the self – but neither is the colour we see provable to be the colour everyone else sees. This is *how* I see it, but also, this is how *I* see it.

Mostly we don't need to reflect on this because we don't experience our *experience*; we experience *that which we experience*. Only when we subsequently reflect on experience does that secondary level of awareness come about and we can ask questions about whether what we have experienced exists. To ask if there is a world 'out there' becomes as useful as asking whether it is possible to go on a journey, while travelling along in a car. External reality does not actually go away if I shut my eyes, and Berkeley's original point, which Johnson's kicking of the stone did not address, was simply that we cannot *know* that it exists when it is not being perceived.

Even being tempted to ask whether there is a world 'out there' suggests that everything can be doubted. But surely there has to be a limit to process of systematic doubt, or we will spiral down into confused ignorance. Towards the end of his life, Wittgenstein turned to questions of certainty and doubt, and came to the conclusion that:

> 'If you tried to doubt everything you would not get as far as doubting anything. The game of doubting itself presupposes certainty.'

Paragraph 115 of *On Certainty/Über Gewissheit*.

In other words, however much you challenge and question things, in the end your questioning has to be based on some conviction which you cannot challenge, a foundation on which everything else depends. In the course of growing up, we gather a body of knowledge, or certainty about life. It shapes the way in which we think, and we check out any new information or experience against it. As Wittgenstein put it most succinctly, 'You need grounds for doubt'.

A fundamental doubt about the existence of the world is something that goes against the basic certainties that we use in our day-to-day living. Not even a philosopher can doubt everything. The world exists; that much we know for certain, not just because it is the basis upon which we are able to doubt other things, but simply because we are part of that world. But the idea of it being 'out there' is itself an illusion, created by the sense that we are located somewhere behind our eyeballs.

Even the most analytic of philosophers, in their daily lives, make assumptions about the world that they cannot justify logically. That is not a failure of their philosophy, but simply recognition that abstract reasoning has its limits. The same brain that is capable of doubting the external world is – at the very same time – busy with all those automatic operations which connect the individual to the rest of the world; we breathe air, we are aware of heat and cold, we move and negotiate our way round things. And our brains have been

might well argue that it merely gives you a starting point, to actualize your luck (or otherwise) you need to use imagination, energy and so on. You have a situation and need to capitalize on it if you are to be successful. Not altogether luck, then; he who dares, wins.

But our circumstances throw up another problem. To understand anything fully (if that were indeed our aim in a well-ordered life that did not depend on chance or luck) we would need to understand everything, simply because everything is related to everything else. So, to take a decision that is completely luck-free, we would need to take absolutely everything into account, but that's obviously impossible. We hit what Heidegger called the 'infinite background' problem – we can never have enough information to make up our minds. At some point we have to jump, to take a chance. Life, as any insurance company will tell you, cannot be risk-free. My fate may be partly predictable – the insurance premium will be based on certain assumptions depending on my age, sex and medical history – but that is only a matter of statistical probability, never certainty.

Does luck therefore let me off the hook? Can I disclaim ultimate responsibility for my decisions, on the grounds that an infinite background of facts has rendered my apparently free choices inevitable, or that the random scattering of events and chances means that my life will always depend on luck rather than effort? Is fatalism the only sane option in a world where chance rules? Or where the rules determining the chances are beyond our ability to know? Perhaps only partly. There is a much-quoted maxim 'chance favours the prepared mind' – used by, among others, Ansel Adams, for making the most of the opportunity to get a good photograph – which may illustrate the benefit of a bit of existential philosophy here. After all, part of our 'beach' exploration in thought has been to consider what we are looking for in life, what we value, what matters most to us, what ambitions we have set ourselves. If we have reflected on all those things, we are prepared to see opportunities to fulfil them once they arise. Not to be sure it's something you want is a sure-fire way to fail to grasp what is offered. So your taking a 'beach' moment of reflection may enhance a sense of direction and prepare you to recognize the value of such opportunities as present themselves.

Nobody succeeds without luck, but no amount of luck guarantees success. The aim is to be alert to what life throws up, to see its potential, and have the courage to go for it. But, for all we may commend ourselves for having made the most of our opportunities, or blame ourselves for having let them slip from our grasp, we may generally console ourselves with the thought that mostly it's down to luck.

So what part has luck played in your life?

AT HOME

Me? Offer advice on what you should do to maximize your chances? You'll be lucky!

27

Have you had your butterfly moment?

In the 4th century BCE, a Chinese Taoist philosopher dreamed he was a butterfly – almost weightless, flitting about effortlessly in the air – but woke to find that he was still the solid, earthbound, human form of Chuang Tzu (or Zhuangzi). But then he asked himself, 'Was I a man dreaming that I was a butterfly? Or am I now a butterfly dreaming that I am a man?'

There is a moment, as we wake, when our dream is still with us but we start to become aware of being in bed, of looking around, and then of 'coming to ourselves' and recognizing the room and the familiar features of our life. In good times, such waking is comforting, reassuring; the bizarre dream – food for an analyst – is receding and we are happy to be back in our normal context. In bad times the painful reality of life comes flooding back; we wish we could remain in our dream.

So how do we distinguish dream from reality? Two concepts may help us: coherence and continuity. We live within a web of relationships and we acquire responsibilities; our waking reality is therefore one that coheres with that of others. We are who we are because other people know who we are; they respond to us and we respond to them. We put things down and later retrieve them; we walk into a familiar room and it remains that same room, it does not morph into a swirling mass of cloud or some alien landscape. In a dream, by contrast, that coherence is lost. Dreams are disjointed, populated by people from different phases of our life, with scenes shifting into one another with a bizarre logic that we cannot follow. We get into a car only to find we are floating down a river, and – a moment later – walking on dry land. If it lacks coherence, it's probably a dream. Waking reality also provides us with continuity; we live, grow, develop, follow a career, have a family. Our memory is reinforced by the tokens of our past that we see around us – people, places and things affirm our identity. We change only slowly, growing and ageing, and are able to remember who we were and how we changed into who we are now. And that continuity applies also to our environment, we observe change, and thereby know that we have lived through it.

So, on the face of it, the question is fairly straightforward. Reality is what has continuity with the past and displays coherence with what we experience in the present. In a dream we lose both continuity and coherence, that is what makes the dreaming experience so vivid and bizarre.

Yet the contrast between dream and reality is not absolute. Our dreams are distinctively ours and, even without the help of an analyst, may reveal aspects of ourselves of which our conscious mind is unaware. Dreams may also reveal our longings, hint at our potential, and introduce us to the possibility of the previously unthinkable. They may also prompt us to ask whether what we take to be our normal, waking self, is an inevitable reality for us or even a desirable one. A dream may show us who we want to be.

There is another kind of dream: a daydream, in which we imagine how things might be for us and try to think outside our habitual box, projecting ourselves into a new context. Coming out of such a dream can also create a 'butterfly' moment to which Chuang Tzu's question is relevant.

Have you had a butterfly moment of that sort? They may happen when we find ourselves in a new and congenial context: the warmth, the food; the wine; the new circle of friends, relaxing without a care in the world. Suddenly the world is easy; we flit from flower to flower. This is the life! We look in local estate agents' windows, dreaming of the whitewashed Greek villa or minor French chateau that could replace our suburban semi. Surely, we argue, we could be tethered to an income stream by no more than an internet connection and laptop; our children could grow up bilingual; our evenings would be spent listening to cicadas rather than commuter traffic. Suddenly a new life seems possible. Then there is the nudge, literal or metaphorical, to remind us that we are dreaming. That the suit, tie and spreadsheet await us, or the domestic routine of getting the kids off to school; that our 'real' life will re-assert itself in a few days; that our reality is not here on holiday but back at home.

Or is it? Ask yourself the Chuang Tzu question. Which is the real me and which is the dream? Is the 'at home' reality inevitable? And if I made a move to something entirely new, would that be simply chasing a dream, or waking up to my full potential?

There are plenty of television programmes to encourage the dream to become waking reality – how to swap your home for one in the sun – but they focus on the practicalities of such a life change. For an exploration of the emotions involved, there is Willy Russell's wonderful monologue (or play, or film) Shirley Valentine, where a frustrated and bored Liverpool housewife takes a trip to Greece, falls in love and finds that her life is transformed. In the middle of that story you are rooting for her, wondering whether she can genuinely find happiness or whether she will get dragged back into her former life. The Shirley Valentine question is also Chuang Tzu's butterfly question – which is the dream and which is reality, and can the one become the other?

To be called a dreamer is hardly a compliment; it implies that fantasy takes precedence over reality. But when it comes to the fundamental questions about who we are, by what values we wish to live and how we order our priorities, it is far from clear what is fantasy and what reality. Long before

Freud, dreams were used as a method of self-discovery, and one person's daydream may be another person's profound intuition that things could (and should) be different. Reason tends to follow experience, favouring caution and continuity; the dreamer takes an unreasonable leap into the unknown, seeking to re-shape life to fit an intuition or a glimpsed possibility. But does that imply the dreamer is unwise?

Chuang Tzu's philosophy may be linked to two broad positions – relativism and anarchy – but both in a positive context. He was an anarchist in that he thought life should develop naturally, with minimum interference from the state. People know what is in their own best interests, they just need the freedom to organize their own life. When things are done in the right way they become effortless. Hence he becomes the unknown patron saint of many modern economic Liberals and Conservatives! He also encouraged relativism (less congenial to Conservatives!) by arguing that in questions of value or judgement there are no absolutes. One person's idea of beauty will be different from that of another, and there is no way to say that one is right and the other wrong. Except of course, like all Taoists, he favours that which is natural. In the philosophical quest to understand life, ancient Taoism is a rich resource.

At some point on this mental or physical 'holiday' from your routine, there is much to be gained from asking the 'butterfly' question. Which of my lives, here or at home, is more real? Am I a banker dreaming that I am a hippy, or was I formerly a hippy dreaming that I was a banker? It is potentially a very dangerous question to ask!

AT HOME

The butterfly story is found in the second chapter of *Chuang Tzu*, which is a compilation of work from the philosopher himself and his followers. For more on Chuang Tzu's philosophy, see my book *Understand Eastern Philosophy*, Teach Yourself Books, 2012.

28

Can you live with impermanence?

If there is one thing that we can know for certain, it is that everything is impermanent and therefore that nothing is certain. The Buddha pointed out (he hardly needed to argue the point, since it is a common feature of experience) that all compound things are subject to dissolution; what has been put together will eventually come apart. That may sound depressing, but it is a simple fact of life – *the* most basic fact of life, with which we would be wise to come to terms if we are to find happiness.

Impermanence dominates every level of experience. Sometimes it hits you immediately as you emerge from the plane: the heat, the unfamiliar language, the sounds and smells of a new environment. You enter a new world, pulling your suitcase of familiar essentials into the unknown. But glance over to the departure lounge and there you can see the crowds of tourists waiting to catch the return flight; that will be you soon, they were you not long ago. You are here to experience, consume and disappear; much like life, but more compressed.

On the cosmic level, we need not worry that the galaxies are flying apart, nor even that Andromeda, with its trillion stars, is heading on a collision course with our own, smaller, Milky Way, for long before they merge and transform this part of the universe, humankind will have disappeared and its Earth along with it. In cosmic terms, our lives last but an instant and are of no measurable significance. Hardly started and yet it's nearly over 'and the place thereof shall know it no more', as *Psalm 103* has it.

In *On Certainty*, Wittgenstein pointed out that a door can only swing open because it has fixed hinges. Our ability to doubt and question rests on some assumption or assumptions that we accept as certain. Similarly, our ability to understand and appreciate the process of change depends on a sense of something unchanging that we can use as a reference point. The problem is that, where life is concerned, even those things that seem most permanent for us will eventually change. Impermanence swallows all.

Perhaps that's why people have found the idea of God so tempting. When all else is subject to change, the idea of a single supreme principle underpinning that change is not just a comfort, but a means of getting an intellectual, moral and personal viewpoint. Those who do not have such a viewpoint might well take a commitment to the abilities of human reason, or a view of human flourishing, to serve the same purpose. Even Buddhist philosophy, for all its recognition of the fundamental process of change and the dissolution of all entities, encourages people to 'go for refuge' to the Buddha, his teaching and the community of his followers. You have to set your fixed point somewhere.

And here's the problem. We may choose to make a person our fixed point (assuming that they will never let us down, or die) or a career (assuming that we will be on the upward trajectory for ever and never retire) or a place, or a set of beliefs, or a political party, or a nation, or an ideology. And yet all of these things are themselves subject to change. Finding permanence is like swimming against a current, however much you try to make progress you realize that you are still being carried away.

Is there any answer to any of this, or do we just give up in despair? How do we live with impermanence?

One possible answer, in an approach encouraged 2,500 years ago by the Buddha, and more recently by those seeking to alleviate the stress of modern living, is to practise 'mindfulness' and thus to engage with the present moment. But experiencing the 'now' is far from easy. We are aware of the passing of time in the tensing of events: this belongs to the past, I remember it and live with the results of it; that belongs to the future, it is what I hope for or fear, and it shapes my choices and plans. And yet we actually inhabit an infinitely shrinking present moment, between the one and the other: pushed by the past, pulled by the future, and easily lost in our preoccupation with both.

The present moment is, however, of the utmost importance: it is the point at which you choose, think, act, celebrate, live. You cannot live in the past; if you try to do so, you simply live disengaged from the present. Nor can you live in the future, for it is yet unformed and the hiding place of hopes and fears that can so easily paralyse present enjoyment. Hence within Buddhist philosophy, being aware of the present moment is not just a philosophical necessity (if we are to be fully awake to what exists, rather than what does not) but also central to the quest to overcome the general dissatisfaction with life to which humans, in their attempt to cling on to things in an impermanent world, are all too prone.

Why? Because, right now, your past and your future are no more than scripts being rehearsed in your mind. The present moment is the only reality, but it is always coloured by the account that you give to yourself of yourself (this is who I have become) and the story you are making up about your tomorrow. It is all too easy to become so obsessed with either or both of those stories that the present (and only) reality is swamped by them. To be thus preoccupied is to deal with what does not exist – either because it has already been and gone, or because it is yet to happen (and may not).

Yet, according to Buddhist philosophy, the present moment is the reality that sums up all the past and shapes all the future. It is the moment of decision and of taking action to shape what will be. From the Buddha to existentialism, the present moment is crucial. New age practitioners encourage us to live in it, meditation helps us to focus on it, yet more often than not it escapes our serious attention.

Children are naturally in the 'now'; watch a small child give attention. Something that fascinates also brings us into the 'now'. We quite 'forget ourselves'; we are 'taken out of ourselves'. In our elation we may shift deities from the Apollo of formal structures and thought to the Dionysius of exuberance (to use the classic distinction between those Greek gods).

The moment of sexual release is certainly a 'now', as is the moment when you launch into the void, tethered to safety only by your bungee, or leap from the plane a moment after the cameraman. The 'beach' moment is also a 'now', an opportunity to bracket out the stories for once and to live on the ever-changing edge of present experience.

Why does that sound so corny? Simply because it may be embarrassing to recognize and acknowledge that the 'touchy-feely', new age, counsellor-inspired, religious, guru-promoted reality may actually be given a sharper intellectual edge. By a rigorous attempt to concentrate on one's present experience – whether by concentrating on the process of breathing, or simply observing the passing play of emotions and thoughts, acknowledging each and allowing them to pass – we achieve a sense of being fully engaged, like a surfer on a wave, where an ever-changing experience tips us forward.

How does living in the 'now' address the problem of living with impermanence? Simply because, according to the Buddha, our dissatisfaction with life comes from our temptation to crave for life to fit our own particular desires – a craving that is bound to be frustrated, for life does not dance to our tune. The 'if only', which may equally be addressed to the past and the future, encourages helplessness; engagement with the present provides opportunities for change. If all things are subject to change, it will always be futile to resist and cling to either the no-longer existing past, or the not-yet imagined future. If we continue to do so (as inevitably we do, most of the time) we should at least be aware of the negative consequences.

There is a Buddhist parable in which a man, fleeing from a tiger, swings himself over a precipice holding onto a wild vine. Hanging there in mid air he looks up to see the tiger watching him. But then he looks down and there below he sees another tiger, waiting for him to fall. Then he looks up again and sees two mice. Bit by bit they are gnawing away at the vine to which he is clinging. Hanging there, he sees a strawberry growing within reach and picks it. How sweet it tastes!

That's you, basically. Enjoy your strawberry!

AT HOME

For those who want to appreciate the 'now' of impermanence, most introductions to Buddhist thought include sections on the practice of mindfulness.

For those determined to take the philosophical hard way to explore how the human being experiences time as tensed and engages with past and future, Martin Heidegger's *Being and Time* addresses these issues.

Or look up Heraclitus, who also explored the nature of change.

29

Is the actor in pain?

The stalls are packed with Humes. Although they don't look much like the 18th-century Scottish philosopher and historian David Hume, the audience are responding as Hume would have expected. As the tragedy unfolds on stage, they become emotionally involved; they are drawn into the action and empathize with the characters, they feel the pain, the emotional turmoil, the helplessness that they read in the expressions of the actors. They display what Hume regarded as a natural human sympathy towards those who are suffering.

Except, of course, the audience is deliberately allowing itself to be conned. There is no pain; the blood on stage is not real. The cries of anguish are perfectly timed to sound authentic, but they have been carefully rehearsed. Murder has not been committed on stage; this is, after all, not a Roman amphitheatre, where anguish was for real and entertainment took on a rather more sinister character. We know, at the moment when the actor is stabbed and writhes on the ground that he or she is not actually in pain. We know it because we have paid to sit in these seats and watch the play, and that there was a matinee performance in which, presumably, a similar scene of anguish was acted out. We also know that this same actor can perform quite differently; can seem to be an utterly different person. Hence, the emotions we feel while watching the action on stage are real enough for us, although our rational mind can detach itself from what it sees and appreciate its context as a good performance.

The perfect actor conveys and evokes emotion by word, gesture, expression and total body language. That is what it means to play-act, to give every external sign of being the character portrayed. The better the actor, the more engaged we become; the more powerful the performance. But what about the world outside the theatre? How do you know whether what you see of another person is a genuine expression of emotional or physical pleasure or pain or simply an act? How can you distinguish genuine from fake?

The fact that you can even ask this question tends to presuppose that each of us comprises an invisible mind controlling a physical body – an ancient view of the human self that was, in the 17th century, expressed in radical form by Descartes. The self is non-physical, theoretically separable from the physical body, whether at death or through out-of-body experiences. It was a view caricatured in the 1950s by Gilbert Ryle as 'the ghost in the machine', and one that has, in more recent times, tended to be replaced by a more materialist, neuroscientific view of the self. We assume that a brain scan, or checking for the presence of endorphins, might show whether the pain was real, and that a lie detector, by measuring tiny physical changes, could check whether the unseen self was being genuine in its external words and actions. But is the data we could get from such tests the same thing as the feelings that the person is or is not having? Presumably not – so we are back to the 'hard' problem of consciousness (see Chapter 15).

Given that we know our own conscious experiences directly, but have to infer those of others from their words and gestures, we cannot be certain of what others experience, especially in a world that includes actors, not all of whom are on stage or screen. I can't believe that you are in pain, because you're a good actor and could well, at this very moment, be fooling me; the boy has cried 'Wolf!' once too often; the constant moaner may at last have something genuine to moan about, I just cannot tell.

Heidegger pointed out that many of us escape from the challenge of being authentic all the time by adopting masks. We act out our role – whether parent, child, employee, benign patron, village idiot – because acting a pre-defined part in life's play is generally easier than writing our own script and taking responsibility for how the play develops. The challenge of the existentialists is to be yourself and face the angst of self-doubt, rather than accept the easier route of sticking on a mask and following the script.

If I choose to adopt a mask, my play-acting is conscious – I say what is expected, but feel nothing – and I can rightly be accused of hypocrisy. But what if the mask is adopted unconsciously? Can I fool myself into feeling something that I would not have felt otherwise? Is it possible for an emotion to be false to the person who actually experiences it? Psychology would generally suggest that is the case; emotional confusion may have an unconscious cause.

It might also be worth reflecting on the way that emotion and behaviour are susceptible to social influences. It is hard not to go along with the emotions of those who surround you in a crowd; not to accept the part that you are given, especially if you are part of a chorus with the security of seeing others performing similarly and on cue. The dilemma of knowing whether the actor is in pain may thus be extended to the issue of moral responsibility for those who are carried along with a political, social or religious ideology. Do they really feel and believe that?

Am I – however unconsciously – acting out a role throughout my life? Was Shakespeare right about all the world being a stage, and therefore that we are all called upon to play parts and act accordingly? Am I more genuine at some times than others? Am I ever completely free from a mask? And, if so, how could I ever unambiguously show that to be the case? The person who claims to be genuine is most likely not to be so.

So we are back to the ambiguity of the theatre. I can never know whether that to which I respond emotionally is genuine or a sham; I cannot observe the consciousness of another person. On the other hand, in order to continue to live with others, I have to make certain assumptions about when they are being genuine and when they are wearing a mask. Sometimes you see a mask slip and a more genuine self is revealed. But there is no guarantee that the self now revealed is actually genuine. There may be other layers of deception. Can I trust you? Can I trust myself? And is the actor in pain?

In the end, given that we are not in a theatre watching a paid performance, there comes a point at which we have to accept the declared emotions of others on trust, albeit without surrendering our critical faculties and while recognizing that we all wear masks from time to time, since being utterly authentic all the time is just too much hard work. The alternative to such trust would seem to involve the constant questioning and challenging of every emotion, in a situation in which there can be no definitive answers, and that way madness lies.

This would seem to imply that Cartesian dualism still has its place – that there is an 'inner' self that is utterly different from the physical body it inhabits. That is a remarkably unfashionable view, in a world where neuroscientism promises a full and exclusive explanation of the self in terms of brain activity, but it seems to me that dualism of some sort is a necessary fiction (if fiction it be) if we are to make sense of the daily authenticity or deceptions of our interpersonal world. And it must remain so until we are all equipped with little machines for getting an instant readout from one another's brains, as a means of checking that the emotions expressed are genuine.

AT HOME

Read *Meditations*, René Descartes, for reflections on the nature of the self from a dualist point of view, or *The Concept of Mind*, Gilbert Ryle, 1949, for a critique of Descartes' view.

Consider what evidence you would need to conclude that someone you know well is not being genuine with you.

Watch your own reactions to a good performance, whether on stage or screen. Can you resist the urge to engage emotionally with what you see?

30

Is reality 'God'?

Pierre Laplace (1749–1827), when asked where God fitted into his account of the universe, famously declared 'I have no need of that hypothesis'. His example is followed almost universally today when it comes to the study of cosmology; supernatural beings are not needed by way of explanation. There is a case to be made for saying that they are not needed for religion either, although observing religion as it is practised, you'd be hard pressed to come to that conclusion.

Earlier we looked at whether Pascal was prudent to bet on God and whether his wager was still relevant. Whichever way you came down in evaluating the various options, one thing is clear – the word 'God' keeps cropping up, and causes much confusion. So let's explore one of the options in more detail – the idea that the word 'God' is simply a shorthand way of speaking about 'reality itself' (whatever that means).

There are two ways of coming at this, one negative the other positive:

- The negative approach is to point out that the idea of 'existence' is incompatible with the idea of a God who is infinite, eternal and therefore present everywhere. That which is everywhere is nowhere. Things are only known by their boundaries; they exist in the literal sense that they 'stand out' in our experience – you can see where they are because you can also see where they are not. With no boundaries, whatever is meant by 'God' cannot be said to 'exist' in the literal sense of that word. On the other hand, following that argument, 'reality itself' does not exist either, since it is not an individual thing with boundaries. So is it possible that 'God' and 'reality itself' refer to the same thing?

- The positive approach is to explore what religious people and philosophers have said about 'God' to see the extent to which they also point to 'reality itself'. St Anselm, an 11th-century French monk who ended up as Archbishop of Canterbury, declared that 'Where God is not, there is nothing', and Martin Luther argued that God was within every living creature. And those views reflect an absolutely central belief of Judaism and Islam as well as Christianity. To attempt to identify 'God' with a physical object is idolatry, the worst of sins. But if God is not to be an idol, then that word cannot refer to something that exists in the same way as anything else. Whatever the existence of God means, it cannot be the hypothesis that there is something to be found somewhere to which the name 'God' applies – that would be idolatry.

Both suggest to me that the word 'God' is an optional, perhaps a useful, way of describing reality, a word that some people find helpful in making sense of the world emotionally as well as intellectually. If so, then 'God' is a cultural construct. But how is it that people think they can claim to 'know' the will of such a god? The very concept of 'will' assumes that, at its most fundamental level, reality takes on human form. Perhaps that's the only way we can understand it, or engage with it emotionally. Humanism suggests that is not the case, and that reason and evidence can provide a perfectly adequate way of engaging with life's intellectual questions.

The reason why it's important, from time to time, to return to this question is that religion shows no sign of going away. It may be bland and uncontroversial, or strident and a threat to secular society and humanist values, but it continues to act in the name of God.

There are two possibilities:

- Either millions of people are deluded into thinking there is a God, use that delusion as a basis for their lives, and are sometimes prepared to die for it. If that is the case, then we need to ask what sort of delusion this can be. After all, humanists and atheists have produced convincing reasons to show that a god cannot exist in any literal sense. They have argued that you can live a good, meaningful life, without using the 'God' concept as a guide. They have argued that religion has caused much strife. And all that may be agreed by at least some religious believers. But the stark fact remains that religious belief not only survives but thrives. That alone is a global phenomenon that needs explanation. Perhaps humankind has some natural predisposition to believe, or religion of some sort gives some evolutionary advantage.
- Or, if it is unlikely that such a large swathe of modern humanity (including many of the most intelligent) is deluded, it must be the case that 'God' can be understood in a way that is compatible with the general matrix of modern ideas.

Forget the caricatures of chocolate teapots and the like! This is one of the most challenging questions we face today. Is it not absolutely crazy that, in the 21st century, opinion is divided – even among the intelligentsia – on a question as fundamental as the existence of God, and the prior question of what 'God' means!

Hence the importance of exploring whether 'God' is best understood as a shorthand way of describing 'reality itself' and engaging with it in a personal way. If we start to see 'God' not as the name of something that might or might not exist, but as a term used for some of the most profound intuitions we have about the reality within which we live, then it makes sense for some forms of religion to continue – indeed it places the religious quest in parallel with the philosophical one, except that the religious quest is accompanied by a range of emotionally engaging activities, rather than relying on reason alone.

Mediation between the religious and atheist fraternities is fraught with problems. Any mention of God not 'existing' and most (but not all) believers will start to square up for an argument. Although if you say that he does not exist in the sense that everything else exists, they will agree with you. (And of course, as has happened here, you find yourself drawn into the trap of using the word 'he' and thereby to slip towards the idea of God as an individual.) On the other hand, suggest that there may be some way of getting a personal appreciation of the heart of reality, and the atheist and humanist fraternity, smelling a religious plot to entice everyone back into a world of superstition, will start to proclaim the benefits of encountering the world on the basis of human reason, uncluttered with any metaphysical trappings.

My personal view is that the problems dividing the two camps are highlighted by considering the claim that: 'God is the creative source of everything'. Two options:

1   Either it is a definition of what we mean by 'God'? If so, there is no problem. The 'source of everything' is what the word 'God' refers to. That same source can also be described scientifically and poetically. Some will find it helpful to call that creative source 'God', others will find that word distracting and will prefer to engage directly with the reality itself.
2   Or that same statement can be taken to mean that 'God' – as known and defined independently in religion – happens to be the creator of everything. Whatever science may show us, and however much physicists at CERN seek to recreate the conditions of the earliest universe, believers know that their God is the real source of everything, and that the universe has to look outside itself for its explanation.

If you take the second option, you are thrown back into the old debate, with Pierre Laplace (and, more recently, Stephen Hawking) claiming that no 'God' is needed to explain the origins of the universe. Of course not! There cannot be a separate, identifiable entity called 'God' which we could identify as the creator! We would need to get outside our whole conceptual box to attempt such an explanation of the universe. But that approach has a long history, summed up by the phrase 'God of the gaps', whereby people assume that some external being called God can come in and explain those gaps in scientific knowledge that we have so far failed to plug. But scientists will soon point out that, even if there is a gap, it is simply a sign of our inability to explain something in scientific terms – it does not imply some sort of 'gap' within the structure of the universe, a gap that requires the special operation of some extra-universal being. That belief is not only illogical and plainly wrong, but it is also religiously inadequate.

If a religion is desperate to locate or give plausibility to its notion of God, it might be tempted to go down that route, but the attempt will only serve to show the very limited nature of its own concepts – whatever 'God' might mean, it surely means rather more than an invention for filling gaps in our knowledge!

So the first alternative is the more promising, and many have taken that route, from Schleiermacher in the 19th century, who described religion as sense and taste for the infinite, to Paul Tillich in the 20th, who – borrowing terms developed by Heidegger – described God as 'Being itself' in order to convey the idea that the word 'God' refers to the framework of our understanding of reality and not with a particular piece of content within that framework. God is not 'a being' but 'being itself'. For me, reading Tillich in the 1960s was a liberation – it freed me to study Theology as a way of engaging with the most profound questions about human life and its place in the universe, without having to surrender to outdated metaphysics. Controversy raged around the publication of *Honest to God*, as even John Robinson, Bishop of Woolwich, dared to admit that our image of God had to change.

The pity is that, once this sophisticated notion of God is removed, superstition takes over, whether it is accepted or rejected, and you are back to the old opposition of the naively religious and the militantly atheist. A sense of awe at the wonders of nature, and intuitions about human life and its values, may be expressed eloquently within music and art, and sometimes these take on a religious character. Philosophers should be able to engage with such things without embarrassment, and without the sense of having to jettison intellectual integrity. But it seems to me that that can only happen if we start from the assumption that the word 'God' is a way of describing reality, not a way of avoiding it.

AT HOME

For a overview of what people mean by 'God' try Karen Armstrong's *The History of God*, Vintage Books, 1999.

For a wonderfully provocative classic that launched the debate about God in the latter part of the 20th century, try *Honest to God*, written by John Robinson, then Bishop of Woolwich, in 1963.

And for a sense of the wonder of nature that does not require the use of God language, but expresses that which has also inspired religious thinkers, read any of Richard Dawkins' books on science and evolution – particularly perhaps *Unweaving the Rainbow* and *Climbing Mount Improbable*. Or, for a sad misunderstanding of the issues, and the tragic polarization that has blocked this discussion for many people, try his *The God Delusion*.

31

Is *pragmatism* useful?

Pragmatism gets things done; it goes for what works and judges the truth and value of ideas on that basis. If there's a choice between ideas or theories, the pragmatist goes for the one that yields the best results, not necessarily the one that is the most accurate or even the most logical. In other words, it goes for what is useful.

In science, theories are held provisionally; if they fail to match up with evidence, or to be fruitful in terms of helping with our knowledge as a whole, then they may be discarded and replaced. If in doubt, go for the best available theory, but be aware that one day it will be surpassed. To take the opposite, absolutist view would be a scientific disaster, implying that an existing theory should be defended to the last, only to be replaced when an alternative could be proved, with absolute certainty, to be right. But, of course, that cannot happen; new theories are always tentative. So it is natural to take a pragmatic approach to the assessment and use of scientific theories. We know that the application of Newtonian physics is limited, and that – as an overall explanation of the universe – Einstein is rather more useful; but that does not stop us using Newtonian physics for solving ordinary problems on the surface of the planet. We know that in extreme conditions light may bend under the influence of gravity, and time and space may be flexible, but when it comes to mundane problems, Newton does just fine. In technology and science, pragmatism is not just OK, it is essential.

John Dewey (1859–1952), a key thinker in the pragmatist movement in the USA, made the important point that knowledge is a problem-solving activity. We think because we need to act, and our thought is therefore embedded in intended action. Knowledge is important, not just for itself, but because we need it in order to live. And this has implications for education from primary school upwards – we use our minds most effectively when we are engaged in solving problems rather than learning facts.

So, from a pragmatic point of view, our thinking needs to be engaged in problem solving, developing theories that are effective and yield results. But there is a bit of conventional wisdom that, when your only tool is a hammer, every problem looks like a nail. Leaving aside it's applications for US foreign policy, or Heidegger's references to a hammer (that most emotionally satisfying of blunt instruments!) as a tool ready-to-hand, it finds a more nuanced expression in – where else? – Nietzsche, who suggested that one hears only those questions to which one has answers. If that is correct, then our thinking is always going to have a pragmatic bias, for we are likely to dismiss as non-questions those to which we can see no possibility of a usable answer. And that, of course, might well be a valid complaint about our last question concerning God and reality! So pragmatism might not just lead us to select the best answers to questions, but also the best questions, judged by whether a workable answer is in prospect. Why strain for the higher branches when there is plenty of low-hanging intellectual fruit?

In its broader sense of opting for that which delivers a practical outcome, pragmatism also seems to be the approach of choice in matters of politics and economics. The politician coming into power and faced with responsibility for governing the country, knows that he or she cannot implement all the exalted promises made while still in opposition – so pragmatic decisions have to be taken, for politics is 'the art of the possible'. But we love the rhetoric of ideals, and hate the compromises into which even the most idealist of politicians is forced eventually to sink. 'He didn't deliver!' is ever the chant of the disillusioned, and idealists berate the pragmatic politician – there should be no negotiation with terrorists, no cuts in public spending, no increases in taxation! Where, the day after the election, is the promised land?

This might well bring a belated smile to the face of the arch-political pragmatist, Niccolo Machiavelli. In his survival advice for an aspiring ruler in 15th/16th-century Italy, based on a lifetime of experience of the political intrigues of his native Florence, he argues that, for the maintenance of power and the coherence of the state, it may well be necessary for the Prince to know how to act ruthlessly. Decisive punishment, carried out ruthlessly but effectively, establishes authority, quells the inclination on the part of the discontent, and brings peace and security. Indecision or kindness, however justified by one's moral principles, can lead to chaos. Political leadership cannot afford such ideals. As a ruler, you must do what is necessary to maintain the authority of the state. If it is possible to act with kindness, then fine; if cruelty is called for, do not hesitate! How do we evaluate that sort of pragmatism?

Similarly, when it comes to matters of the heart, pragmatism is less appealing. Would you wish to be pragmatic in love? In friendship? In marriage? To be pragmatic about such things implies a cold, calculating, unfeeling approach to life. Not in love, but taking a pragmatic view of the prospect of marriage? Hardly the stuff of romance! To be pragmatic in matters of friendship verges on the cynical. There are some areas of life where compromise in order to achieve a practical result feels like the failure of a dream rather than a policy of choice.

So how do we get a useful and workable (pragmatic!) view on pragmatism itself? Sitting on your beach, philosophizing, it is all too easy to dismiss the compromises of everyday pragmatism and determine to follow a dream. Ideals generally appear at their most attractive when contemplated from a safe distance; whereas pragmatic compromises are seldom the stuff of legend or personal self-congratulation. Unfortunately, however, uncompromising idealists are, more often than not, a pain to friends and family. Pragmatists are able to compromise, to blend in, to play their part without causing too much grief. Philosophers are not exempt from the antisocial tendencies of the determined idealist, and the life of reason does not necessarily result in a reasonable life. If you are tempted to assume that great thinkers automatically qualify for a calm, rational, principled *modus vivendi*, just read *Philosophers Behaving Badly*. Those who refuse to compromise on their ideals, or their ambitions, sometimes produce wonderful results, and the domestic and personal chaos that comes with such determination doesn't in itself detract from the quality of their thinking, but you have to ask yourself whether you'd want to be married to any of the great philosophers in that book, or have them as a parent or child.

So pragmatism reveals a fundamental split between the rational and emotional aspects of life. In the rational world of calculation, anticipated results, political and social options, pragmatism is the antidote to the chaos of idealist fanaticism; in this world where compromise is the norm, pragmatism delivers. But in our personal life, in our dreams, our highest aspirations, we generally want to go beyond pragmatism. Nobody strives to be second best, or dreams of being moderately successful. Aspiring to take the practical option sounds like a contradiction. So is pragmatism useful?

AT HOME

Read *The Prince* by Niccolo Machiavelli (Penguin Classics, 2003 or other editions) or any of John Dewey's work on pragmatism.

Pragmatists to Google: C. S. Pierce (1839–1914); William James (1842–1910) and John Dewey (1859–1952).

Or, if you are more interested in the unconventional aspects of philosophers, try *Philosophers Behaving Badly*, by Nigel Rodgers and Mel Thompson, Peter Owen Ltd., 2005.

32

How did you become who you are?

There's nothing quite like a break away from routine to initiate questions about how we have become who we are. By what process do we generate character? Can we/do we change fundamentally, or only superficially? Am I simply a weathered version of the child I remember being? Are we born with such an overwhelming genetic inheritance that our character traits are as determined as the colour of our eyes? If it were so, siblings would share such traits, which is not necessarily the case. Can I put everything down to circumstances and the effect on me of events beyond my control? Possibly, but there again, people react in different ways to the same situation, so there must be some other, internal, factors that made me respond to life in the way that I did. It would be nice to understand that process – because then we'd know what to blame!

Let's take stock. We know that we change as we go through life. But we also know that certain personal features are established very early on, others develop later. As we evolve from childhood to old age, we see the world differently; new things become important for us, new values are established. We measure up to the expectations of family responsibilities or work; we mellow into grandparenthood or retirement. Some remain young at heart; others become prematurely old. If you doubt the curious balance between personal continuity and change, just log on to Friends Reunited!

So what is the process by which the self is shaped? This is a huge subject, so I intend to introduce just one image which I find helpful to make sense of that process: mapping.

As you look out from that imagined place of identity between your eyes, you see a world that is already populated with people and places that you recognize. (Although, if you are at this moment sitting on a featureless beach a thousand miles from home, it might be better to visualize a more cluttered and familiar scene!) In your imagination you can fly in all directions, locating places homely or remote, people who are important for you or best avoided, things you value, things you hate. In other words, the world as you encounter it is full of value and significance, and this value is mapped out over the physical world. You see something and either like it or dislike it for your own particular reasons – and each new experience will be informed by everything that has happened in your past, and will go on to inform your future. And the longer you live, the more you encounter the world, the more complex will be the set of memories and values that colour your experience.

You are, in effect, creating a map, superimposed over the world of your experience; a map showing value and significance. Some very general features will have been established on that map from an early age. They show the rise and fall of the ground and can change (if they change at all) only very gradually. Other features are more recent, they are mapped over the existing contours, rather as semi-transparent overlays are placed over an existing map. For some, the early contours are so sharply defined that they continue to dominate the map. Others will find that subsequent overlays are so significant that the original contours are moulded almost beyond recognition.

And as we live, so we grow this map. It is there as we wake in the morning and travels with us throughout our day.

Features of significance pop up in front of us as we encounter them. After all, it's not necessary to remain conscious of all the features of our life all the time. We use our map rather as we would Google information; we encounter something and our internal search engine relates it to our past experiences. I smell coffee and immediately that smell has associations: coffee beans being roasted in a shop that I regularly passed as a child; sitting down and sharing a break with friends; relaxed conversations over coffee at the end of a meal; a friend who always valued good coffee, and encouraged my younger self to experiment beyond the instant spoonful. All of this happens – consciously or (mostly) unconsciously – the moment someone suggests stopping for a cup of coffee, or I get a quick whiff on the morning air.

The engine for all this mapping is, of course, memory. If you lose your memory, even for a moment, you don't know who you are or how to relate to the world around you; you are utterly lost. Finding yourself again is finding that you have regained the map of your life.

This 'map' image helps us to get round the old difficulties concerning the nature of the self with which we started. Are we formed by nature or by nurture? How much of who we are is genetic, and how much is determined by our growing up and later experience? Could we eventually be known entirely through neuroscience? In other words, is there a model of ourselves imposed in some way over our brain, such that we could be known and analysed entirely in terms of the physics of neural activity?

If the process of developing as persons follows the analogy of mapping, we can appreciate both nature and nurture equally. What we are is partly established before birth (we do, after all, inherit much from previous generations and some things from the whole of the animal world); we happen to be human. That says more about how we will go on to map out our world than anything else. But then, from the first opening of our eyes, the first discovery of a mother's breast, the first recognition of a human face above us as we lie in our cot, we start to map – this is pleasant, I want more of it; that is painful, get me out of here! And the baby cries, and learns and cries again. It is already developing personality; it is learning to engage with its world. And as memory tracks this engagement, its personal map is being drawn.

On this theory, personal identity is no more located in a single point in the brain than information on the web is located in a single computer. Rather, it reflects an on-going interaction between the conscious self and its world, an interaction that uses memory to inform and colour every aspect of that encounter. The old person, sitting quietly and reflecting, is zooming (as on Google Earth) over the mapped terrain laid down by memory, a terrain that is utterly personal, including millions of bits of experience set out in relationship to one another. The map is not seen all at once; parts may be quite forgotten until some stimulus brings it to mind.

Sadly, for those who develop dementia, the map starts to fail; connections are not made; the face is seen but not recognized. 'I really can't place you!' 'I've no idea where I am!' The earliest contours of personality may remain for a while, but the later overlays have gone.

In dreams, the map becomes jumbled. Often the terrain over which we pass in a dream is vaguely familiar – the room plan of a house in which we have once lived, perhaps. But superimposed on it are people from quite other periods of our life. A corner of our office is suddenly transformed into a childhood den in the garden. Grandparent and grandchild may appear together in spite of years that separate the death of one from the birth of the other. Our map is jumbled. But then, on waking, we 'come to ourselves', we recognize where we are and who we are.

It is that experience of 'coming to yourself' that denotes a re-engagement with our map. We are located again in the mapped world of significance. We may suddenly feel reassured and comfortable, or sick with the recognition of our predicament; either way, we are back into the process of mapping.

One of the most productive features of being away on holiday is that, by engaging with a new set of experiences, we are expanding and refining the contours of our map, so that, on returning home, we see the familiar with slightly changed eyes.

Read *Me*, Mel Thompson, Acumen, 2009 for an exploration of different aspects of the self and the process of mapping.

Or try *The Ego Trick* by Julian Baggini, Granta, 2011.

33

Do you own your own thoughts?

It's obvious that you own your own thoughts. How can anyone else lay claim to them? The fact that you can keep your thoughts to yourself is sufficient proof of ownership. But in a world of copyright and copyright theft, where public interest is cited as a valid reason to publish private conversations, and where information – whatever its source – is regarded by some as public property, your thoughts may not remain exclusively yours for long.

What is it that you can genuinely claim as your own? After all, when you speak, think or write, you use words and concepts that – unless you have just created a new word and are about to explain it – you have gathered from the various communications you have received from the world around you. Your thoughts may be uniquely yours, but only in the sense that you have put words and concepts together in a form that has not existed before. Without the whole tradition of thought and language, you would be unable to communicate. So there is a real sense in which we do not 'own' our own thoughts, we simply borrow and re-shape the thoughts of others. Creation is transformation. We do not create from nothing; that activity was traditionally ascribed only to God. So if you have what you judge to be an original idea, should you claim it as your property? Or does it belong to everyone? Are you simply an agent acting on behalf of the whole community of people whose language you share?

Copyright is yours in the sense that you have taken from a common cultural pool and made something unique from it – indeed, the general rule in dealing with manipulation of images is that you can claim something as your own copyright if the creative input that you have given is more significant for the final result than the original on which you have worked. The question is whether you have done enough to claim the final result as yours.

Intellectual property is the general term for things that people claim as their own: words, ideas, creations on stage and screen, artworks of all kinds. IP is valuable. You can sell the right to copy your work, you can earn royalties on your books, images or music. IP is all about design, innovation, creativity. Every new product emerges with IP attached, and in some areas (the production of new drugs, for example) the investment in research means that the intellectual element is far more costly than the final production process. IP represents a substantial percentage of a nation's Gross Domestic Product. If you give away your IP without expecting any financial return, how will you fund your next line of research? IP is big business.

Should you simply give everything away for nothing? There is a strong lobby today for all information to be freely available once it is in the public domain. The web is full of good stuff, freely distributed. But that does not mean that it has no value, quite the contrary. It has value, since people want it, but it comes as a gift from its creator. But it remains a gift, not something that the recipient should subsequently claim to have received by right. So when people argue that everything should be made available for free, they are really saying that everyone should give away what they have created, rather than try to make money from it.

Is that simply a matter of generosity rather than greed? You may decide to make your thoughts freely available on the web, but the risk is that you thereby undermine the market for books and magazines that offer the same for a price, and on which others depend for their living. Is it not indulgence to be able to give away what others depend on for income? In a parallel context, the same might be true of any volunteer, whose services enable the number of paid staff at an organization to be reduced.

The problem is that all IP comes at a price, even if it is mainly the time and effort on the part of the creator. If it is then offered free, the concept of professional creation becomes nonsense; if there is no money to be made out of intellectual property, then there will be little incentive to create. If every new design can be ripped off and produced more cheaply elsewhere, what hope is there for original creation?

There was less of a problem when everything bought and sold was a physical product, but how do you contain the situation when everything can be transmitted and reproduced in digital form? How do you assess the value of a product that can be copied an indefinite number of times?

Some ideas can't effectively be copyrighted. Take the basic idea of how you operate a supermarket. It transformed shopping. The idea of walking into a store, picking up a basket and helping oneself to the goods was quite revolutionary, saving time, effort and cost. It was tried, found to work well, and universalized. Yet we open supermarkets today without thinking of paying a royalty to those who first developed them. Was Herr Diesel ever fully rewarded for the design of his engine, or Monsieur Biro for his ballpoint pen? And should the descendents of Thomas Caxton not be receiving something from the generations who have used printing presses? Or Thomas Crapper for the flush toilet? After all, if you had to pay a penny every time you spent one, the descendants of Thomas Crapper would have been more than compensated for the misuse of their name.

By contrast, Bill Gates' fortune flows from the licensing of his software products; his ideas are protected and he is constantly being rewarded. But what then of the free software that does almost exactly the same thing? Should we all opt for that instead, and deprive Mr Gates of his royalties? In a fast-moving innovative world, it is difficult to know exactly who invented what; things offered for free may have borrowed from what costs, and vice versa.

So should you opt for the 'everything is free' view or do you go against the trend in some quarters and insist on legitimate copies of everything, so that the creator is rewarded? Take the first option and you threaten the future of commercial creativity; take the second, and you have to admit that most creators borrow from others, and you can never be sure that everyone is rightly rewarded.

This issue is reflected in the modernism/postmodernism debate in philosophy and culture. For the modernist, the creative self is key. Extending a tradition that goes back to the Enlightenment idea of the autonomy of the individual, or the Reformation notion that each person should be free to interpret and believe according to conscience, the thinking individual became paramount. By contrast, the postmodernist world sees the creator as a monkey gathering fruit in a cultural jungle, proudly displaying his or her fruit bowl but hardly willing to claim any one item in it as exclusively his or her creation. Everything happens within a social and cultural complex of ideas and media. We never work in a vacuum, and the media shape the content they offer. You can no more think in isolation than play football in isolation. Without the team, no game; without a social and linguistic context, no thoughts or words. How can you claim anything as your own?

So, whether you want to try to protect them, or give them away for free, you still need to ask yourself the basic question, 'Do I own my own thoughts?'

AT HOME

If you have borrowed this book, or found it lying discarded on the beach by someone despairing of philosophy, please consider buying your own copy when you get home!

34

Are you well connected?

We are mortals with portals, and we guard them closely. Have you noticed the way some people never answer the phone but respond immediately to text messages? They are in control of their communication system, free to decide whether, how and when to respond. Indeed, sending a text or email rather than phoning may serve to acknowledge respect for the recipient's time. It suits the fast pace of modern life. It asks 'Is this communication convenient right now?'

While some portals are guarded, others become a means of opening up to the world – log on to a social networking site and it is like entering a room in which a party is in full swing. Suddenly you are told quite intimate things by people with whom your connection has previously involved no more than a perfunctory click of the mouse. It's all there; it's all happening; be part of it!

At the other end of the connection scale, clicking the 'unsubscribe' link is an act of self-affirmation in the face of the torrent of information from commercial sites concerned that you should continue to feel wanted as a loyal supporter. It is sometimes hard to say 'no' when someone, or some organization, wants to make contact. We are bombarded with information as if our brains were databases desperate to be populated. Connectedness is the norm; the standalone computer is the ageing exception to the networked world; soon we will need no more than a simple portal through which to access our work, entertainment and relationships on the cloud. It may be – as Nicholas Carr has argued in *The Shallows* (Atlantic, 2010) – that the web encourages us to skim over the surface of things, absorbing information at a great rate, rather than understanding it in depth. If so, it may have implications for the way we connect with other people. If we surf the web for superficial information, what of the friendships it might offer us?

Communication has always been a central feature of human life, without which civilization and security would not be possible, but digital communication has increased the speed, range and quantity of communications to a point at which it needs to be monitored carefully if it is not to get out of hand. And nowhere is this better illustrated than in the question of friendship and how many friends it is possible or sensible for a person to have.

There are many studies exploring the nature of friendship, but a good starting point is Aristotle's view of friendship in Books 8 and 9 of his *Ethics*. He claims that 'Nobody would choose to live without friends even if he had all the other good things.' Friends are also a refuge when poverty strikes or things go wrong. Possession of many friends is one of the greatest things in life. But he distinguishes between three kinds of friendship:

* Friendship based on utility – the person with whom you are on friendly terms because either you perform a service for them or they offer you service. (Those who are ambitious may well cultivate friends in strategically important places. Those who want their business to thrive will cultivate their customers with gestures of friendship.)
* Friendship based on amusement or leisure activities – there are shared interest groups for almost everything, and sharing a common passion binds people together. (However, such friendships seldom outlive an ending

of the original thing that brought people together. You give up the sport, leave the club, and the friendships you cultivated there wither.)

* Friendship for its own sake – according to Aristotle, this is the hardest to establish and yet is also the most long lasting. The person I have as a friend accepts me for myself, and I accept him or her for what they are. They are a person with whom I wish to spend time; in whose company I feel I can be genuinely myself.

Aristotle makes the point that a key feature of friendship is that you wish your friends well for their own sake, not simply because they are your friends. If you love someone because they are good company or offer you some benefit, that cannot be genuine friendship, because such love actually refers to the self, not to the other. Collecting friends can be a selfish business.

Even if it is possible to attract plenty of people on the basis of mutual utility or pleasure, and such 'friendships' take little time or effort, he makes the point that genuine friendship implies the desire to spend time in one another's company. Once that kind of friendship is established, separation does not negate it – I meet my friend after a long absence and it is as if we had never parted.

In Section X of Book 9, he asks the crucial question for 21st-century digitally enhanced friendship – 'How many friends should one have?' The optimum number, according to Aristotle, is 'the largest number with whom one can be on intimate terms'. In other words, you cannot really share friendship with a large number of people; if genuine friendship requires time in one another's company, the number of friends that any one person can have will be limited.

Aristotle would not accept the mouse click that confirms you are now friends with someone whose name and face you only vaguely recognize – a friend of a friend, as you try to locate them on the outer reaches of your personal 'map' – as a sign of true friendship. One tweet doth not a friendship make, neither does the mutual hitting of the 'like' button confirm serious interaction. Social networking transfers into the personal sphere techniques developed for business, where mutual support and keeping lines of communication open with potential customers is essential. The problem, it seems to me, is that it leaves a slight ambiguity in the supposed friendship – they're telling me about their new book or other product, but does that mean I'm a friend, or a potential customer, or both? Time in one another's company tends to self-select genuine friends; time online blurs the categories.

That is not to dismiss the value of social networking sites or the hugely improved way in which we can now connect with one another. To Skype across the globe enables a degree of intimacy and an immediacy of conversation that previously would have only been possible face to face. Neither should we doubt that the written communication – even if limited in its number of characters – can establish close friendships, as was often the case in days that treasured the hand-written letter. But the sheer quantity and brevity of much online communication must make its 'friendships' questionable from Aristotle's perspective.

So how does this impact on your experience of the beach? If on holiday, you may have a pile of cards to write – the 'wish you were here' that may or may not mean what it says. The postcard is the most controllable of media; the older equivalent of the text message in terms of length. But the thing about postcards is that they cannot be replied to directly. When did you ever put the hotel address on a card anticipating a reply? Postcards simply express our willingness to be connected, but leave you in control. How very modern that old form of communication seems!

You may have your smartphone turned on – in which case your connectedness will have reached your 'beach' retreat, and you will already have had opportunity to establish the quality of friendships or the degree to which you are regarded as indispensable at work.

You are known by and through your connections, and just as a computer gets 'cookies' downloaded to it from other computers wanting access and information, so we receive personal 'cookies' from the web; people influence us through the access we give them to our personal virtual space. Our portal is open, whether friendship is likely to come that way is quite another matter. So are you well connected?

AT HOME

Read Mark Vernon's *The Meaning of Friendship* (Palgrave Macmillan, 2010) or Aristotle's *Ethics* for more on friendship.

Reflect on your chosen means of communicating with friends, and on the number of friends with whom you can manage to have a close relationship.

35

Who were you?

Most people are dead. Death is the norm; it is life that is the rare exception. And it gives us relatively little comfort to recognize that we will be entirely recycled (whether we choose burial or cremation). We know that the atoms of which we are made were fashioned five billion years ago in the centre of an exploding star and that they will go on for billions of years more. We appreciate that we are but their temporary arrangement into human form. But we can't actually identify with any of that; we are ourselves only in so far as we are conscious, and the question 'Who were you?' – a question that we will never live to be asked or able to answer – hovers over the boundary of our experienced sense of self. It was the question implied by all myths of a final judgement, with threats of hell or the promised rewards of heaven, as we are required to give an account of ourselves before some higher power. 'Who were you?' is the question that gives conventional religion its power. It is the question about ultimate value and purpose and about whether something as temporary as a human being can have any meaning within the greater scheme of things.

Epicurus (341–270 BCE) dismissed concern about death, since 'when we are, death has not come and when death has come, we are not', a view echoed in the 20th century by Ludwig Wittgenstein. That may not entirely produce the tranquil acceptance of death that Epicurus sought, since I would judge the final moments of life equally to be feared.

Even if you believe that the self survives death in some way, you are still never going to be in a position to be asked 'Who were you?' since if you survive death you presumably continue to be. As a matter of logic rather than religious vision, survival of death is self-contradictory.

Yet many, including some great thinkers, have tried to minimize that perspective. In the 19th century, the ethical philosopher Henry Sidgwick became one of the co-founders of the Society for Psychical Research, whose presidents included William James and Henri Bergson, both substantial philosophers. There was a widespread hope that science would somehow help to deify humankind, offering a promised immortality. There was a fascination, that continues in some parts to this day, in attempting to show that the dead still live – even if their communications from beyond the grave appear rather limited and banal. Yet surely that approach if it goes beyond what can be proven scientifically, is a form of escapism.

It may indeed be essential to argue that a finite human life has a valuable and permanent place within the overall scheme of things (in other words, from an 'eternal' perspective), if we are to commit to values that transcend the individual. We are parts of a whole, and are valued as such. But that is not the same as trying to claim that, as individuals, we continue to live (or have the potential to live again, if our mummified or deep-frozen remains can be resuscitated). To argue that death is somehow unreal, or temporary, is to go against the very nature of living things. We are compounded, made up of endless cells that live, grow and die. We are a process that had a beginning in conception and will have an ending. The whole nature of living things depends upon death and change. We are not the same as we pass through life; how much less likely that we can become a living fossil after death?

But whether or not – for reasons religious or intellectual – you believe in life after death, consider for a moment the perspective on this present life that death offers. We are bounded by death and defined by our own finitude; we live knowing that we will die. It is a thought from which, for most of the time, we will do anything to escape. Yet a holiday, like sex, offers a 'little death', or at least a temporary death (a holiday limbo between who you were and who you want to be), a non-orgasmic letting-go of our ordinary life, allowing ourselves to luxuriate in the present moment. And, hopefully, after the holiday, we can go back and start life afresh, or at least refreshed in our post-holiday reincarnation.

As we stand back (or sit back, or relax back) on our 'beach' and look at life, the perspective of our own death has a great deal to offer. Here, for example, are three thoughts from the *Meditations* of Marcus Aurelius, who managed to combine philosophy with ruling the Roman Empire in the second century:

The first is that death is a great leveller:

> *'In death, Alexander of Macedon's end differed no whit from his stable boy's. Either both were received into the same generative principle of the universe, or both alike were dispersed into atoms.'*
>
> **Mediation 24, Book 6.**

(That said, it is assumed that the stable boy did not die over the course of a couple of days from what might have been poison, following a long night of drinking and partying, interspersed with baths and a chance to take a nap. The manner of one's dying may vary according to rank and circumstances, even if the end result does not.)

The second is that death is essentially a letting go from the constant drive of life:

> *'Death: a release from impressions of sense, from twitchings of appetite, from excursions of thought, and from service to the flesh.'*
>
> **Mediation 28, Book 6.**

(But one might also say that, albeit to a lesser extent, of old age.)

And the last puts death in the context of the constant process of change in life:

> *'Observe ... how transient and trivial is all mortal life; yesterday a drop of semen, tomorrow a handful of spice or ashes. Spend therefore these fleeting moments on earth as*

Nature would have you spend them, and then go to your rest with a good grace, as an olive falls in its season, with a blessing for the earth that bore it and a thanksgiving to the tree that gave it life.'

Meditation 48, Book 4.

Why is it that 'I did it my way' is such an empowering line, however it is crooned into the microphone? Simply because the emphasis is on the 'my'. Unfortunately, few of us will be able to say that with integrity on our dying breath. All through life we tend to ask 'Who am I?' and, by implication 'What may I become?' The future is the open zone of hope that the limitations of the past may be overcome. There comes a point when we no longer have that future. We start to ask 'Why was I?', attempting to make some sense of life as a rounded whole.

Sartre famously declared that 'Hell is other people' towards the end of his play *No Exit*, about three people who find themselves together in hell, spared conventional means of torture but allowed to torment one another. It highlighted a more general feature of his thinking, namely that we are always afraid of being defined by others, limited by them. We rebel against being pigeon-holed. We know we are more than people see of us at this minute; we know they misunderstand our intentions and fail to appreciate our thoughts. Yet we can hope to change, to explain ourselves better, to defy expectations. But at death, the attempt to escape the opinion of others ceases; we have no more chance to defend ourselves. We cannot stand up and contradict what is said at our funeral oration. We are stuck with what we are seen to have been by others. Death is the perspective we most fear; in the face of it we are defenceless, our record fixed for others to interpret.

The mistreated dead cry out for vengeance – a theme in much literature and art, from ancient legends to modern films. Life has a value that is not always appreciated: we want it to be; we want them to have the last word. We want them, as we want ourselves, to be understood and for the truth to be known. We sense that we are not just what others see; that our story, from birth to death, is not all that can be said about us; that we aspired to be something more, that life was an inevitable compromise that we secretly regret. Perhaps the greatest fear of death is the fear of believing that one has not fully lived, however long or short one's life.

Death makes life manageable. If we were immortal there would be too many choices, too many careers to follow, too long to give us an excuse for not perfecting everything we do. Given an infinite period of time, we would all equal one another, all study everything, all engage in everything – gradually tending towards a bland perfection. It is death, finitude, the recognition that we have one life to choose, live through and take responsibility for, that gives us character. Death is the perspective that gives our life its individual meaning.

John Donne's famous lines 'Ask not for whom the bell tolls, it tolls for thee' encapsulate the existential approach to death, namely that the fact of death places a question mark over all our lives. And the reason, as he presents it is that 'no man is an island', we are part of a common humanity, bounded by death. Anyone's death, but particularly those close to us, forces us to consider our own life and mortality. We are who we are because of the fact of death.

There are accounts of philosophers being 'philosophical' in the face of death, of whom Socrates and David Hume are perhaps the best known, and Bertrand Russell spoke of death in terms of a river finally flowing out into the sea, which is fair enough as an image, but only for those dying gently in old age. But the problem is that the events that end in death may also be random, untimely and merciless. In the traumatic situation of those facing the certainty of imminent death, some seek to make some final gesture that sums up their sense of self – as we heard in heart-wrenching calls from the mobile phones of those trapped in the upper floors on the morning of 9/11. Equally, the condemned may react strangely to the threat of death, perhaps wanting to die well, to maintain their self-respect to the last. Faced with death, some see only the ridiculousness of the living – all ideas explored in a wonderful short story by Sartre – *The Wall* – about the reactions of three men condemned to death in the Spanish Civil War.

So that's it: not what I will become, but what I have done and what I am now; the final perspective.

AT HOME

Read Jean-Paul Sartre's short story *The Wall* or his play *No Exit*.

Browse gravestones in a cemetery or churchyard. Not as morbid a task as you might imagine; it becomes a celebration of human life in all its variety – from the long-lived paterfamilias to the infant whose life hardly started, and from the wealthy, much respected and lauded in stone, to those whose memorials give little more than a name and dates. All life is here, family by family, side by side.

Understand Existentialism in the Teach Yourself series explores the personal implications of death in the thoughts of Heidegger, Sartre, Camus and others.

There is also a book on *Death* in Acumen's *Art of Living* series, which explores philosophical themes in an accessible, personal and relevant way.

Postscript: Time to kick away the ladder?

Infants can have a wonderful time let loose on a computer keyboard. Slapping keys at random, with a bright colour and large font pre-selected for them, they chuckle to see how their actions create funny patterns on the screen. Innocent of all understanding of words, meanings, punctuation, they have no notion that what they are creating is other than patterns of colour and shape. Years pass and they struggle, first with one finger, then two, to type words. In adulthood, many never feel the need to get beyond that stage, happy to carry out a fast process of transcribing ideas or scribbled notes into glowing text, nodding up and down as they check screen against keyboard. A touch-typing course moves that to a new level, and eventually the experienced typist can convey ideas and text to the screen without stopping to think where the individual keys are located. QWERTY becomes the unnoticed background to the activity of typing; thought is directly instantiated in the movement of fingers. Ask me where the 'n' key is located and I have to stop and think, but I can type 'think' without thinking.

No surprise there, for the same process can be seen in those who learn to play an instrument, drive a car, learn a foreign language or take to the dance floor. Conscious thought and deliberate manipulation is a necessary stage on the way to a much faster, more fluid, unselfconscious action.

Reflective thought, the distinctive feature of humankind and the essence of philosophy (or should that be the essence of humankind and the distinctive feature of philosophy?), is therefore a transitional stage between recognizing that there is an issue or problem that interests us, and engaging with it in a natural and spontaneous way. Take the problem of consciousness and the nature of the self. Before we embark on philosophy, we take the existence of other people for granted, and we assume we know what it is to be someone. With the arrival of philosophy, we puzzle over whether the mind is distinct from the body, whether it is instantiated exclusively in the brain, whether we are the same person over time as we grow older, whether we can ever know another person directly. We live with a range of questions, seeking to answer them in a way that is logically coherent. But when we set aside our philosophizing and get back to the business of dealing with other people, our responses to them (unless we have become a serious case for treatment) are natural and do not consciously refer back to our earlier arguments about the self.

So that's the sequence: first we live intuitively; later we stop and think, weigh up options, analyse what is around us; finally we live intuitively once again. But – and it is a big 'but' – the final intuitive state is not the same as the first; for it has absorbed into itself the result of our thinking. Even if we do not rehearse it, it is there.

No experience is pure, all is coloured by our own mental and emotional mechanisms. Our engagement with life is therefore informed by clear thinking or by muddled thinking. I am not claiming here that only those who consciously engage in philosophy are able to think clearly – far from it; philosophers are as prone to muddles as anyone else, and insight does not depend on a knowledge of the history of ideas.

Zen insight may arise spontaneously, but that does not mean that Zen practitioners do not have to spend years in disciplined training. If 'chance favours the prepared mind', then philosophy is a good preparation for maximizing your chances of insight and effective action.

But when thought becomes reflective, it starts to dissect its own operation. It examines its own logic, it refines its processing of sensations, it questions its meanings. Did I really see that, or was it an illusion? Was I right to conclude X on the basis of Y? The problem is that there can develop a feedback loop in this self-reflective process; mind feeds on mind feeding on mind. Logic chopping is a mental black hole into which the intellect can sink. Nothing wrong in that, I suppose, if it's what you enjoy – but it may not answer questions posed by the real world.

Even if logical analysis has its limits, thinking is not only analysis, but also attention. It is attention to the process of experience and response, to the way in which we value and assess our situation. It is checking whether decisions actually match our considered values and aims, and therefore whether they will, in the long run, achieve what we want. It is, in short, the examined life. And once life is examined, one of the features of that examination should be the recognition that not everything can be appreciated or understood in logical terms.

At the end of his famous early work *Tractatus*, Wittgenstein – having argued that philosophy is an activity rather than a body of knowledge, and that its task is the clarification of propositions rather than the accumulation of facts, so that our thoughts have sharp boundaries and do not lead us astray – used a remarkable image for the process of philosophizing. He said that the person who has gained clarity through philosophy 'must, so to speak, throw the ladder away after he has climbed up it' (*Tractatus* 6:54).

That image can serve for much philosophy. Without philosophy we can be easily fooled by the words we and others use, we may make unnecessary assumptions and fail to clarify exactly what we mean. The propositions of philosophy serve to elucidate, to enable us to gain clarity. But once we have used them for that purpose, they are best set aside. They are not ends in themselves.

There are fundamental questions about life that cannot be resolved simply on the basis of clarification. Neither can science give us all that we need to sort out the confusions of life. Wittgenstein argues that, even if all the questions of science had been answered, the problem of life would remain completely untouched. He then says, quite remarkably, 'The solution of the problem of life is seen in the vanishing of the problem' (6:521).

There are things that can become clear to us, but cannot be stated in propositions. The important thing is to recognize which questions can be answered and which cannot, and to know that there is an end to all this asking.

Some may think that Nietzsche has featured rather too much in this book. His writings are at times enigmatic, bizarre, offering glimpses of wisdom rather than coherent argument, and as a thinker, he is human, all too human, and his insights are as much psychology as philosophy. Yet he is a good starting point for those who, settled on their beach for a bit of reflection, want to probe the existential questions of life and its meaning. One comment, made in *The Gay Science*, is particularly apposite as we draw this extended holiday reflection to a close. He argued that our thoughts are but shadows of our feelings, simpler and darker. Our emotions are frequently complex and, if we are honest with ourselves, may often betray hidden and perhaps conflicting values. Our thoughts, on the other hand, are the attempt to simplify and rationalize those feelings, to construct a view of the world that makes sense of what we accept as, or hope to make, our chosen values.

There is plenty of opportunity for self-delusion; the neatly organized, rational view of the world is seldom an accurate portrayal of the mixture of emotions that bring it to birth. Nowhere is this clearer than in debates about religion – the anger and frustration displayed equally by religious believer and militant atheist are sure signs of confused emotions. If in doubt, shout louder, so that you may feel the force of your argument!

So there are limits to what philosophy can offer. The life of reason may feel cleaner, less cluttered, more purposeful, but in itself it cannot solve those deeper issues of value and meaning that are experienced emotionally before they are articulated. That requires the simpler (but far more difficult) task of just sitting, watching and noting the interplay of feelings and thoughts.

Wiggle your toes in the sand again. Shut your eyes and let the sun burn orange discs through your shades. You simply are, you exist, you – on the surface of this planet at this moment – are something of a mystery, a bundle of questions not all of which are answerable. Breathe deeply and allow the ideas and then the book itself to slip from your grasp. There comes a time when every philosopher should recognize that enough is enough.

Index

Understand the Philosophy of Religion: Teach Yourself

Mel Thompson

This book is for anyone wanting to understand what religion is really about. Exploring all the key principles upon which religion is based and setting out the arguments for and against belief in a clear, accessible style, it examines religion against current issues such as terrorism, evolution, and our multi-cultural society.

Paperback
£12.99

ISBN: 9781444105001

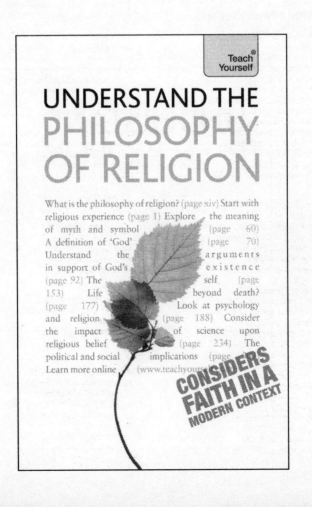

Teach® Yourself

UNDERSTAND THE
PHILOSOPHY
OF RELIGION

What is the philosophy of religion? (page xiv) Start with religious experience (page 1) Explore the meaning of myth and symbol (page 60) A definition of 'God' (page 70) Understand the arguments in support of God's existence (page 92) The self (page 153) Life beyond death? (page 177) Look at psychology and religion (page 188) Consider the impact of science upon religious belief (page 234) The political and social implications (page Learn more online (www.teachyour

CONSIDERS FAITH IN A MODERN CONTEXT

Understand Philosophy: Teach Yourself

Mel Thompson

This book is the essential introduction to the history of Western thought. Covering the key thinkers, both ancient and modern, and the major branches of philosophy, it will give you new insights about the world we live in. Packed full of examples and clear explanations of key terms, it is ideal whether you are a student looking for a quick refresher or just want to explore this fascinating topic out of personal interest.

Paperback
£12.99

ISBN: 9781444104998

Teach® Yourself

UNDERSTAND
PHILOSOPHY

What is philosophy? (page x) The theory of knowledge (page 1) Be a sceptic (page 27) Science and philosophy (page 34) Philosophy and psychology (page 58) Explore language and logic (page 68) Meet Plato and Aristotle (page 89) The concept of mind (page 103) Question free will (page 117) Faith, reason and belief (page 138) Does God exist? (page 130) Miracles (page 171) Look at ethics (page 184) Marx and materialism (page 226) Think about human rights (page 237) Get to grips with existentialism (page 246) Learn more online (www.teachyourself.com)

CUTS THROUGH THE JARGON

Understand Ethics: Teach Yourself

Mel Thompson

Whether you're a student studying philosophy at any level, or simply want to gain a deeper understanding of this fascinating subject, Understand Ethics is an accessible introduction to the key theories and thinkers. Fully updated, this latest edition includes contemporary examples and discussion of current debates including terrorism, genetics and the media, helping you to grasp how ethics applies to life today.

Paperback
£12.99

ISBN: 9781444103519

Teach® Yourself

UNDERSTAND ETHICS

What makes something moral? (page 2) The art of living (page 13) Understand freedom (page 16) Get to grips with ethical language (page 35) Are we naturally good or bad? (page 64) Egoism and hedonism (page 71) Utilitarianism (page 76) Conscience (page 91) Nietzsche (page 110) Humankind, Marx and Freud (page 119) Crime and punishment (page 136) Religion and morality (page 151) Learn to cast a sceptical eye over morality (page 175) Applying ethical theories (page 188) War and peace (page 212) Medical issues (page 232) Business ethics (page 256) Learn more online (www...

CONSIDERS CONTEMPORARY ISSUES